불교영어

초급 2

대한불교조계종 교육원 불학연구소 편찬

조계종
출판사

일러두기

○ 본서의 영문본은 한글본과 일대일 대칭의 번역이 아니다.
○ 일부 불교용어 및 문장은 초보자의 이해를 돕기 위해 완곡하게 표현하거나 부분적으로 표현하였다.

금년 연초에 발간한 《불교영어초급Ⅰ》에 이어 《불교영어초급Ⅱ》를 펴내게 되었습니다. 세계화시대를 맞이하여 영어로 불교를 포교해야 하는 시대임을 절감하고 있습니다. 그리고 각종 행사와 모임, 템플스테이 등에서 외국인 불자들과 일반인들에게 한국불교를 소개하거나 불교를 소재로 한 대화를 나눌 일이 많아졌습니다. 본 연구소에서는 이러한 일상적 만남에서 필요한 불교 관련 내용을 영어로 담아내는 작업을 꾸준히 진행하고 있는데, 이번에 그 두 번째의 결실을 맺게 되었습니다.

이 책의 내용과 주요 구성은 기존의 《불교영어초급Ⅰ》에서와 마찬가지로, 크게 3부분으로 구분하여 1부에서는 〈영어회화〉를, 2부에서는 〈불교교리〉를, 3부에서는 〈한국불교 역사와 문화〉를 다루고 있습니다. 그리고 각 본문 사이에 쉬어가는 코너인 〈지대방 이야기〉 편에서는 선시와 찬불가를 영역하여 수록하였습니다.

1부 〈영어회화〉 편은 사찰에서 일상적으로 가장 많이 접하는 주제와 상황을 6개의 장으로 나누고, 각 장마다 가능한 대화 상황을 6단원으로 수록하였습니다. 대화의 주요 내용은 템플스테이, 사찰 안내, 다양한 내용의 전화 통화, 불자들의 여러 가지 수행, 성지순례의 과정들, 한국불교의 문화와 사찰음식 등을 다루고 있습니다. 2부 〈불교교리〉 편은 제법의 분류와 실상, 불교의 여러 가지 수행법, 대승불교의 상징인 보살의 길 등을 다루고 있고, 3부 〈한국불교 역사와 문화〉 편은 불교의 명절, 의식용 경전과 법구, 사찰건축, 우리 불교의 문화유산 등을 다루고 있습니다.

이 책은 승가대학 스님들의 교재로도 활용되기에 대화의 주체와 내용들이 스님들 중심으로 엮어져 있는 것이 특징이기도 합니다. 이 교재가 승가대학의 스님들뿐만 아니라 여러 불자들이 영어로 한국불교를 소개하고, 불교를 포교하는 데 많은 도움이 되기를 기대합니다.

앞으로 매년 출간될 《불교영어중급Ⅰ》《불교영어중급Ⅱ》《불교영어고급Ⅰ》《불교영어고급Ⅱ》에도 지속적인 관심을 가져주시길 바랍니다. 끝으로, 본문에 게재된 사진과 그림들은 조계종불교문화사업단에서 도움을 받은 것임을 밝혀두는 바입니다.

2556(2012)년 9월
대한불교조계종 교육원 불학연구소

Unit

1부 〈영어회화〉 편은 스님들이 사찰에서 일상적으로 가장 많이 접하는 주제를 6개의 장으로 나누고 각 장마다 가능한 대화 상황을 6단원으로 수록하였습니다. 6개의 주제는 템플스테이, 사찰안내, 불교의식, 사찰생활, 수행, 한국불교 역사와 문화입니다.

Words and Phrases
문법 정리와 어휘 활용법

본문과 관련된 내용의 문법을 한번 더 정리하면서 그와 관련된 다양한 표현의 회화를 익히도록 했습니다. 핵심 문법 패턴을 외워 여러 상황의 단어를 활용해보면 자연스러운 대화가 완성될 것입니다.

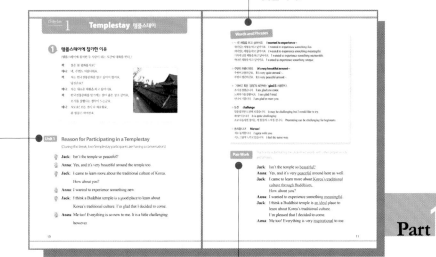

Pair Work 말하기

한글 회화와 영어 회화, 그 단원에 쓰인 단어와 구문의 해설, 그리고 파트너와 함께 관련 회화를 더 연습할 수 있는 'pair work'입니다. 단어와 구문의 경우 되도록 스님들의 환경에 맞는 것으로 수록하여 더욱 효과적인 학습을 기하였습니다.

'pair work'에서는 밑줄 친 부분을 다른 단어로 대체하여 동일한 문장을 지루함 없이 자연스럽게 암기가 가능하도록 하였습니다.

Part 1

지대방 이야기

한숨 돌리고 머리를 식히며 불교문학과 만나는 공간입니다. 아름다운 찬불가와 마음속 깊은 여운을 남기는 선시를 감상하는 공간으로 잠시 휴식을 취하도록 하였습니다.

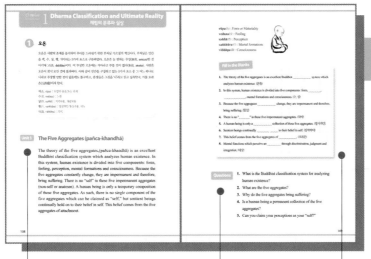

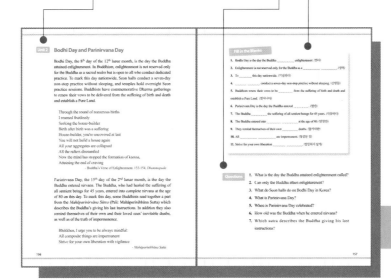

Unit 각 주제에 해당하는 설명

2부 〈불교 교리〉와 3부
〈한국불교의 역사와 문화〉에서는
기본적으로 알아야 할 주제를
선정하여 먼저 한글 지문,
그에 해당하는 영어 지문을
실었습니다.

Questions 질문

본문에서 배운 내용에 대한 질문을
주고받는 상황입니다.
이 부분은 학생들끼리 연습해도
되고 또는 선생님과 학생이 질문을
주고받아도 됩니다. 핵심패턴을
익혀 그 의미를 확실하게 전달할
수 있도록 하세요.

Fill in the Blanks 빈칸 넣기

본문의 주요 부분을 발췌하여
빈칸에 알맞은 단어를 찾아
넣도록 하였습니다. 이는 방금
배운 본문을 복습하는 동시에
주요 단어를 한 번 써보며 다시
익히도록 한 것입니다.

Contents

Part 1 English Conversation 영어 회화

Chapter 1 Templestay _ 템플스테이

Unit 1 Reason for Participating in a Templestay 템플스테이에 참가한 이유   12

Unit 2 Following the Schedule 일정 소화하기   14

Unit 3 Meditation Time 명상 시간   16

Unit 4 Hiking 산행   20

Unit 5 Making Lotus Lanterns 연등   22

Unit 6 Rubbing a Sutra 경전 탁본   26

Chapter 2 Touring the Temple _ 사찰 안내

Unit 1 Buddhas and Bodhisattva at the Main Buddha Hall 법당의 불보살   28

Unit 2 Temple in the Mountain 산사   32

Unit 3 Communal Life 대중생활   34

Unit 4 The One Pillar Gate 일주문의 의미   36

Unit 5 Monastic Life Preserves Nature 사찰생활의 자연보존   38

Unit 6 The Meaning of the Lotus Flower 연꽃의 의미   42

Chapter 3 Conversations over the Phone _ 전화로 대화하기

Unit 1 An Inquiry about the Temple Location 사찰 위치 문의   46

Unit 2 An Inquiry on Transportation to the Temple 사찰 교통편 문의   50

Unit 3 Having a Phone Conversation with a Seunim 스님과의 통화   52

Unit 4 A Phone Inquiry about Templestay 템플스테이 문의 전화   56

Unit 5 Calling to the USA 미국으로 전화하기   58

Unit 6 Invitation to an Event 행사에 초대하기   62

Chapter 4 Buddhist Practice _ 불자들의 수행

Unit 1 Copying Sutras 사경   66

Unit 2 On the Day of the Dharma Gathering 법회 날   68

Unit 3 Prostration Practice 절 수행   70

Unit 4 Cleaning (Communal Work) 청소(운력)   74

Unit 5 Offering Lanterns to the Buddha 등 공양   76

Unit 6 Prayer 기도   78

Chapter 5 Buddhist Pilgrimages _ 성지 순례

Unit 1 Buddhist Pilgrimage Announcement 성지 순례 안내   82

Unit 2 Participants' Questions 참가자의 문의사항   84

Unit 3 On the Morning of Departure 출발하는 날   86

Unit 4 Conversation with a Dharma Friend Sitting Next to You
옆자리 도반과의 대화   88

Unit 5 At a Highway Service Area 휴게소   90

Unit 6 Arrival at the Temple 성지 도착   92

Chapter 6 Korean Buddhist History and Culture
한국불교의 역사와 문화

Unit 1 Millennial Temples 천 년 고찰   94

Unit 2 The Vegetarian Diet of Buddhist Monks 사찰음식   96

Unit 3 Korean Buddhist Temple Food Spreading to the World
세계로 전파되는 한국 사찰음식   98

Unit 4 Daseon-Ilmi (The One Exquisite Flavor of Tea and Seon) 다선일미   100

Unit 5 Monastic College 승가대학   102

Unit 6 Lay Buddhist College 재가불자들을 위한 불교대학   104

Contents

Part 2   Buddhist Tenets 불교 교리

Chapter 1 Dharma Classification and Ultimate Reality
제법의 분류와 실상

Unit 1 Reason for Participating in a Templestay (pañca-khandhā) 오온   108

Unit 2 Impermanence [Anicca] 무상   110

Unit 3 Suffering [Dukkha] 고   112

Unit 4 Non-Self [Anatta] 무아   114

Unit 5 The Four Noble Truths 사성제   116

Unit 6 The Noble Eightfold Path 팔정도   118

Unit 7 The Twelve Links of Dependent Arising (paticca-samuppada) 십이연기   122

Chapter 2 Buddhist Practices _ 불교의 수행법

Unit 1 Meditation (Ahbhāvana) 명상   126

Unit 2 Samatha and Vipassana 사마타와 위빠싸나   128

Unit 3 Ganhwa Seon 간화선   130

Unit 4 Sutra Reading 간경   132

Unit 5 What is Yeombul? 염불   134

Unit 6 Types of Yeombul 염불의 종류   136

Unit 7 Mantra Recitation 진언   138

Chapter 3 The Way of Bodhisattva _ 보살의 길

Unit 1 The Four Immeasurable Minds 사무량심   140

Unit 2 The Four Great Vows of Bodhisattva 사홍서원   144

Unit 3 Who Are Bodhisattva? 보살은 누구인가?   146

Part 3 The History and Culture of Korean Buddhism
한국불교의 역사와 문화

Chapter 1 Buddhist Holidays _ 불교의 명절

    Unit 1 The Day the Buddha Came and Renunciation Day 부처님오신날, 출가재일 152

    Unit 2 Bodhi Day and Parinirvana Day 성도재일, 열반재일 155

Chapter 2 Ceremonial Sutras and Dharma _ 의식용 경전과 법구

    Unit 1 The Thousand Hands Sutra and the Diamond Sutra 천수경, 금강경 158

    Unit 2 The Heart Sutra and the Amitabha Sutra 반야심경, 아미타경 161

    Unit 3 The Four Dharma Instruments 사물 164

    Unit 4 The Moktak and the Seon Stick 목탁, 죽비 167

    Unit 5 Monastic Robes: Gasa and Jangsam 가사, 장삼 169

Chapter 3 Temple Architecture _ 사찰건축

    Unit 1 The One Pillar Gate and the Gate of Non-Duality 일주문, 불이문 172

    Unit 2 The Diamond Gate and the Gate of Heavenly Kings 금강문, 천왕문 175

    Unit 3 Buddhist Painting 불화 178

    Unit 4 Stupas and Seungtaps (Monks' Stupa) 탑, 승탑 180

    Unit 5 Stone Lanterns and Wind Bells 석등, 풍경 183

Chapter 4 Buddhist Cultural Heritage of Korea _ 우리 불교문화유산

    Unit 1 The Tripitaka Koreana and the Janggyeong Panjeon at Haein-sa Temple

        해인사의 팔만대장경과 장경판전 186

    Unit 2 Gyeongju's Bulguk-sa Temple and Seokguram Grotto

        경주의 불국사와 석굴암 189

    Unit 3 The Lotus Lantern Festival 연등축제 193

Part 1

English Conversation
영어 회화

Chapter 1 | Templestay _ 템플스테이

Unit 1 　Reason for Participating in a Templestay
　　　　템플스테이에 참가한 이유
Unit 2 　Following the Schedule 일정 소화하기
Unit 3 　Meditation Time 명상 시간
Unit 4 　Hiking 산행
Unit 5 　Making Lotus Lanterns 연등
Unit 6 　Rubbing a Sutra 경전 탁본

Chapter 2 | Touring the Temple _ 사찰 안내

Unit 1 　Buddhas and Bodhisattva
　　　　at the Main Buddha Hall 법당의 불보살
Unit 2 　Temple in the Mountain 산사
Unit 3 　Communal Life 대중생활
Unit 4 　The One Pillar Gate 일주문의 의미
Unit 5 　Monastic Life Preserves Nature
　　　　사찰생활의 자연보존
Unit 6 　The Meaning of the Lotus Flower
　　　　연꽃의 의미

Chapter 3 | Conversations over the Phone
전화로 대화하기

Unit 1 　An Inquiry about the Temple Location
　　　　사찰 위치 문의
Unit 2 　An Inquiry on Transportation to the Temple
　　　　사찰 교통편 문의
Unit 3 　Having a Phone Conversation with a Seunim
　　　　스님과의 통화
Unit 4 　A Phone Inquiry about Templestay
　　　　템플스테이 문의 전화
Unit 5 　Calling to the USA 미국으로 전화하기
Unit 6 　Invitation to an Event 행사에 초대하기

Chapter 4 | Buddhist Practice _ 불자들의 수행

Unit 1 　Copying Sutras 사경
Unit 2 　On the Day of the Dharma Gathering
　　　　법회 날
Unit 3 　Prostration Practice 절 수행
Unit 4 　Cleaning (Communal Work) 청소(운력)
Unit 5 　Offering Lanterns to the Buddha 등 공양
Unit 6 　Prayer 기도

Chapter 5 | Buddhist Pilgrimages _ 성지 순례

Unit 1 　Buddhist Pilgrimage Announcement
　　　　성지 순례 안내
Unit 2 　Participants' Questions 참가자의 문의사항
Unit 3 　On the Morning of Departure 출발하는 날
Unit 4 　Conversation with a Dharma Friend Sitting
　　　　Next to You 옆자리 도반과의 대화
Unit 5 　At a Highway Service Area 휴게소
Unit 6 　Arrival at the Temple 성지 도착

Chapter 6 | Korean Buddhist History
and Culture _ 한국불교의 역사와 문화

Unit 1 　Millennial Temples 천 년 고찰
Unit 2 　The Vegetarian Diet of Buddhist Monks
　　　　사찰음식
Unit 3 　Korean Buddhist Temple Food Spreading to
　　　　the World 세계로 전파되는 한국 사찰음식
Unit 4 　Daseon-Ilmi (The One Exquisite Flavor of
　　　　Tea and Seon) 다선일미
Unit 5 　Monastic College 승가대학
Unit 6 　Lay Buddhist College
　　　　재가불자들을 위한 불교대학

1 템플스테이에 참가한 이유

(템플스테이에 참석한 두 사람이 쉬는 시간에 대화를 한다.)

잭: 절은 참 평화롭지요?

애나: 네, 주변도 아름다워요.

잭: 저는 한국전통문화를 알고 싶어서 왔어요.
당신은요?

애나: 저는 새로운 체험을 하고 싶어서요.

잭: 한국전통문화를 알기에는 절이 좋은 장소 같아요.
오기를 잘했다는 생각이 드는군요.

애나: 저도요! 모든 것이 다 새로워요.
좀 힘들긴 하지만요.

Unit 1 Reason for Participating in a Templestay

(During the break, two Templestay participants are having a conversation)

Jack: Isn't the temple so peaceful?

Anna: Yes, and it's very beautiful around the temple too.

Jack: I came to learn more about the traditional culture of Korea.
How about you?

Anna: I wanted to experience something new.

Jack: I think a Buddhist temple is a good place to learn about
Korea's traditional culture. I'm glad that I decided to come.

Anna: Me too! Everything is so new to me. It is a little challenging
however.

○ ~ 한 체험을 하고 싶어서요   **I wanted to experience ~**
재미있는 체험을 하고 싶어서요.   I wanted to experience something fun.
의미있는 체험을 하고 싶어서요.   I wanted to experience something meaningful.
기억에 남을 체험을 하고 싶어서요.   I wanted to experience something memorable.
색다른 체험을 하고 싶어서요.   I wanted to experience something unique.

○ 주변이 아름다워요   **It's very beautiful around ~**
주변이 조용하군요.   It's very quiet around ~.
주변이 평온하군요.   It's very peaceful around ~.

○ '기쁘다' 혹은 '긍정'의 표현에는 '**glad**'를 사용한다.
오시길 잘했습니다.   I am glad you came.
노력하기를 잘했어요.   I am glad I tried.
만나서 기쁩니다.   I am glad to meet you.

○ 도전   **challenge**
힘들겠지만 도전해 보겠습니다.   It may be challenging but I would like to try.
꽤 힘이 듭니다.   It is quite challenging.
초보자들에겐 절하는 게 힘들게 느껴질 겁니다.   Prostrating can be challenging for beginners.

○ 동의합니다!   **Me too!**
저도 동의합니다.   I agree with you.
저도 그렇게 느끼고 있습니다.   I feel the same way.

Pair Work   Practice by substituting the underlined words with other proper words and phrases.

Jack: Isn't the temple so <u>beautiful?</u>
Anna: Yes, and it's very <u>peaceful</u> around here as well.
Jack: I came to learn more about <u>Korea's traditional culture through Buddhism.</u>
How about you?
Anna: I wanted to experience something <u>meaningful.</u>
Jack: I think a Buddhist temple is <u>an ideal</u> place to learn about Korea's traditional culture.
I'm <u>pleased</u> that I decided to come.
Anna: Me too! Everything is very <u>inspirational</u> to me.

② 일정 소화하기

(템플스테이 참가자들이 일정에 대한 소감을 나누고 있다.)

잭: 지금 몇 시에요?

애나: 9시 반이요.

잭: 와, 집이었다면 아직도 편히 자고 있을 텐데…

애나: 맞아요. 그런데 벌써 예불, 108배, 아침공양까지 마쳤어요.

잭: 저는 벌써 하루를 다 보낸 기분이에요.

애나: 저는 템플스테이가 아니라 서바이벌 게임에 온 것 같아요.

잭: 우리 탈락하지 말고 끝까지 잘해 냅시다.

애나: 좋아요.

Following the Schedule

(Some of the Templestay participants are sharing their feedback on the program schedule)

Jack: What time is it?

Anna: It's nine thirty.

Jack: Wow, if I was home, I would still be sleeping…

Anna: You are right! But, we've already attended the Buddhist ceremony, done 108 prostrations, and even had breakfast.

Jack: I feel like I am done for the day

Anna: I feel like I'm at a boot camp and not a Templestay.

Jack: Let's make sure we make it to the end.

Anna: You got it!

○ '내가 ~라면 ~했을 텐데' 라고 말할 때엔
  현재에 대한 반대 가정 **If I + 과거, I would~**
  과거에 대한 반대 가정 **If I + 과거완료, I would have + P.P** 라고 표현한다.

  시간에 맞춰 떠나지 않았다면 교통 정체에 걸릴 뻔했다.
  If I hadn't left in time, I would have been stuck in traffic.

  확인하지 않았다면, 예약이 취소될 뻔했다.
  If I hadn't confirmed my reservation, I would have lost it.

○ 벌써 ~을 했다 **already ~** (과거형 동사 + 명사)
  벌써 아침을 먹었다. I already ate breakfast.
  벌써 운동을 끝냈다. I already finished the exercise.
  벌써 책을 읽었다. I already read the book.

○ 좋아요 (동의할 때) **You got it**
  좋은 생각입니다! It sounds great!

○ ~을 가지고 있습니까? **Do you have ~?** (Have는 여러 가지 방식으로 쓰이는 동사이다.)
  몇 시입니까? Do you have the time?
  절에 오는 길을 알고 계십니까? Do you have the directions to our temple?
  제 전화번호를 알고 계십니까? Do you have my phone number?

○ 확실하게 하다, 반드시 하다 **Make sure ~, Be sure ~**
  나는 반드시 주어진 일을 끝낼 것이다. I will make sure to finish my task.
  개인 수건을 반드시 가져오세요. Make sure to bring your own towels.
  우리가 머물던 자리는 반드시 치우도록 합시다. Let's make sure we clean up after ourselves.
  스님의 설명을 반드시 따라주세요. Please make sure to follow the seunim's instructions.

Pair Work

Jack: Do you have the time?

Anna: It's half past nine.

Jack: Wow, if I was home, I would still be in bed.

Anna: You said it! But, we've already participated in the Buddhist ceremony, done 108 prostrations, and even eaten breakfast.

③ 명상 시간

스님: 여러분들은 대체로 참선 초보자니까 먼저 호흡명상을 해보도록 합시다.

애나: 스님, 명상은 왜 하나요?

스님: 명상을 하면 마음을 고요하게 유지할 수가 있어요.

그래서 실생활에도 매우 도움이 됩니다.

애나: 아, 고요한 마음이 되면 안정되어 바른 생각을 할 수 있겠군요.

스님: 그리고 우리나라에서는 화두를 참구하여 깨치는 간화선 수행이 대표적입니다.

쉽게 말하면, 부처님이나 조사가 하신 진리의 말씀 중 하나에 의문을 가져

온 정신을 집중하여, 그 의심을 해결하는 겁니다.

애나: 그럼 보통 어떤 화두를 들죠?

스님: 사람에 따라 다 다르답니다. "이뭐꼬(이것은 무엇인가)?" "나는 누구인가?" 등등

애나: 저도 한번 해보고 싶군요. 그래서 명상과 간화선의 차이를 직접 느껴보고 싶어요.

Unit 3 ## Meditation Time

Seunim: Since most of you are beginners in meditation, let us practice breathing meditation first.

Anna: Seunim, what is the purpose of meditation?

Seunim: If you meditate, you can keep your mind peaceful and calm. Therefore, meditation helps you in daily life.

Anna: Aha! When our minds become calm and settled, we can attain right thought.

Seunim: Exactly. Korea's most eminent meditation practice is Ganhwa Seon, which requires observing a hwadu. In simple language, you arouse a doubt on a phrase originally uttered by the

Buddha or the patriarchs and penetrate it with single-minded concentration.

Anna: Then, what are the hwadus practitioners usually take up?

Seunim: It depends on each practitioner, but more frequently used hwadus include "What Is This?" or "Who Am I?"

Anna: I'd like to give it a try. I want to experience the difference between Ganhwa Seon and other types of meditation.

Words and Phrases

○ ~의 목적은 무엇인가요?　**What is the purpose of ~?**
이 사찰을 설립한 목적은 무엇인가요?　What is the purpose of establishing this temple?
이 프로그램에 참여한 목적은 무엇인가요?　What is the purpose of participating in this program?
이 장치의 목적은 무엇인가요?　What is the purpose of this equipment?

○ ~은 ~에 도움이 된다　**~ is helpful for ~**
독경은 평정심을 유지하는 데 도움이 된다.　Reading sutras is helpful for inner peace.
절은 건강을 유지하는 데도 도움이 된다.　Prostrations are also helpful for keeping fit.

○ ~때부터, ~한 김에　**Since** (접속사)
스님은 1985년부터 명상을 해오셨다.　Seunim has practiced meditation since 1985.
이 전통은 신라시대부터 내려오는 것입니다.　This tradition has been carried down since the Silla period.
아침에 일찍 일어난 김에 산책을 나갔다.　Since I got up early today, I went for a walk.
일찍 도착한 김에 사찰을 둘러보시겠어요?　Since you arrived early, why don't you look around the temple?
지난 토요일부터 이곳에 와 있었어요.　I've been here since last Saturday.

○ 지난~　**Last ~**
지난주.　Last week.
지난 수요일.　Last Wednesday.
예약은 지난주 금요일에 마감되었습니다.　Reservations were due last Friday.

○ 다음~　**Next ~**
다음 주.　Next week.
다음 화요일.　Next Tuesday.

○ 신청서는 다음 날 접수될 겁니다.　**The registration form will be submitted the next day.**

Pair Work

Seunim: Since most of you don't have <u>years of experience in</u> meditation , let us practice <u>sitting</u> meditation first.

Anna: Seunim, what is the <u>reason for practicing</u> meditation?

Seunim: If you meditate, you can <u>maintain</u> your mind in peace and calm.

Anna: So it will <u>lead</u> you to think positively?

Seunim: Yes, meditation is very <u>useful</u> in everyday life.

밤마다 부처를 안고 자고

밤마다 부처를 안고 자고 아침마다 함께 일어난다
앉으나 서나 같이 따라다니고
말할 때나 잠자고 있을 때나 행동거지를 함께 한다
털끝만큼도 서로 여의지 않음이 그림자와 같으니
부처가 가는 곳 알고자 할진대
다만 이 말소리로다.

_쌍림 부대사

Every night
I sleep embracing the buddha

Every night I sleep embracing the buddha.
Every morning I awake together with the buddha.
Whether sitting or standing, the buddha is with me.
Whether talking or silent, the buddha acts with me.
Like a shadow, we are never apart.
Do you want to know where the buddha is going?
Just listen to this talk.

_By Ven. Shuanglin Fu

4 산행

스님: 이제 모두들 비로봉으로 출발하겠습니다.

잭: 등산하며 운동을 하는 건가요?

스님: 예, 몸을 움직이며 신선한 공기를 마셔 보세요.

애나: 저는 들꽃을 감상할 거예요.

잭: 저는 계곡물에 발도 담글 거예요.

스님: 다 좋지요. 그런데 걸을 때에도 알아차림을 잊지 마세요.

애나: 네? 좀 자세히 설명해주세요.

스님: '알아차림'은 곧 알아차리는 마음입니다.

걸을 때에도 '지금 여기'에 마음을 두라는 겁니다.

그러니 몸의 느낌과 걸음걸이에 주목해보세요.

이것을 '걷기명상'이라고 합니다.

Unit 4 **Hiking**

Seunim: Everyone will now head out to Birobong.

Jack: Are we exercising while hiking?

Seunim: Yes. Let's have some fresh air while exercising.

Anna: I am going to enjoy seeing the wildflowers.

Jack: I would like to wash my feet in the mountain stream.

Seunim: Those are all great ideas. However, don't forget to maintain mindfulness while walking.

Anna: I beg your pardon? Would you explain more?

Seunim: Mindfulness is a state of mind that stays alert and aware.

While you are walking, place your mind in the "here and now."

Pay attention to how your body feels and how you walk.

We call this "walking meditation."

○ ∼으로 출발하겠습니다   **We will head out to ∼**

○ ∼을 할 거예요   **I am going to** 동사
할머니를 뵈러 갈 거예요.   I am going to visit my grandmother.
선물을 사러 갈 거예요.   I am going to buy presents.
휴식을 취할 거예요.   I am going to rest.

○ 이것을 ∼라고 합니다   **We call this** 명사
이것을 김치라고 합니다.   We call this gimchi.
이것을 사찰음식이라고 합니다.   We call this temple food.
이것을 경전이라고 합니다.   We call this a sutra.

○ 이해가 가지 않거나 상대방의 말을 듣지 못했을 때, 정중하게 되묻는 질문은 다음과 같다.
다시 말씀해주시겠습니까?   I beg your pardon?
다시 한 번만 말씀해주시겠습니까?   Could you repeat that one more time?
네? 뭐라고 하셨나요?   Excuse me?
다시 말씀해주세요.   One more time please.

○ ∼하는 동안   **While** 동명사
나는 요리를 하는 동안 음악을 듣는다.   I listen to music while cooking.
식사를 하는 동안은 묵언을 해야 합니다.   You must keep noble silence while eating.
템플스테이에 참가하는 동안 마음이 편안해졌어요.
My mind became peaceful while participating in the Templestay.

Pair Work

Seunim: Everyone will now <u>go to</u> Birobong.

Jack: Are we exercising <u>through</u> hiking?

Seunim: Yes. <u>Try to</u> breath in fresh air while moving.

Anna: I am going to enjoy <u>seeing the trees and the landscape</u>.

Seunim: Those are all <u>wonderful</u> ideas. However, <u>don't forget to stay</u> aware while walking.

Anna: <u>I am sorry</u>. Would you <u>repeat that one more time?</u>

Seunim: Being mindful is a state of mind that maintains awareness.
While you are walking, <u>have</u> your mind in the "here and now."
<u>Be mindful of</u> how your body feels and how you walk.
<u>This is known as</u> "walking meditation."

⑤ 연등

스님: 자, 지금부터 연등을 함께 만들어봅시다.

이것이 완성된 연등입니다.

잭: 와! 색채도 화려하고 모양도 예쁩니다.

애나: 정말 연꽃 같아요.

스님: 이제 등을 만들어봅시다.

먼저 종이컵을 바르게 놓으세요.

꽃잎 아래쪽에 풀을 바른 후 컵 가장자리에 한 줄로 붙이세요.

애나: 꽃잎 5개를 붙이니 첫째 줄이 완성되었어요.

스님: 좋아요. 그럼 둘째, 셋째 줄을 붙이세요.

애나: 꽃잎이 얇아서 조심해야겠어요.

스님: 네, 맞아요. 풀을 너무 많이 묻히면 꽃잎 종이가 뭉개져버려요.

그래서 조심해서 다루고 풀을 적당히 발라야 한답니다.

그 아래쪽으로 녹색 잎을 두 줄로 더 붙이면 드디어 연등이 다 완성된답니다.

Unit 5 Making Lotus Lanterns

Seunim: Let's make some lotus lanterns together.

This is what a finished lantern looks like.

Jack: Wow, it's so colorful and beautiful!

Anna: It looks like a real lotus flower.

Seunim: Now, it's your turn to make the lanterns.

Put your paper cup in the upright position.

Put some glue on the bottom of the flower petal.

Stick them on the edge of the paper cup in a single row.

Anna: I finished the first row after gluing five flower petals.

Seunim: Good. Now, keep going with gluing the second and third rows.

Anna: I should be very careful. The petals are very thin.

Seunim: You are right. If you put on too much glue, it will smudge the paper flower petal. So, you have to treat them very carefully and put on the right amount of glue. If you glue on two more rows of green leaves below, you will be done.

Words and Phrases

○ 당신이 ~을 할 차례입니다   **It's your turn to** 동사
당신이 발표할 차례입니다. It's your turn to present.
당신이 노래할 차례입니다. It's your turn to sing.
당신이 요리할 차례입니다.   It's your turn to cook.

○ 계속 ~하다   **keep** '동사 원형 + **ing** (동명사)'
계속 걷다. keep walking.
계속 읽다. keep reading.
계속 보다. keep watching.

○ 접시를 조심해서 다루세요   **Treat the plates carefully.**
손님들을 예의를 갖추어 대하세요. Treat the guests with respect.

○ 끝내다   **finish**
다 끝냈나요? Are you finished?
5시까지 끝내야 합니다. We have to finish by 5 o'clock.

○ 완성하다   **complete**
프로젝트를 완성하기까지 5년이 걸렸다. It took five years to complete the project.
새로운 기숙사는 2016년에 완공될 것입니다.
The construction on the new dormitory will be completed in 2016.

○ 똑바로   **straight**
등을 펴고 똑바로 앉아주세요. Please sit up straight.
여기서 똑바로 100미터를 걸어가면 해우소가 보입니다.
If you walk straight ahead about 100 meters, you will see the bathroom.
여기서 똑바로 보이는 곳이 대웅전입니다.
What you see straight ahead from here is the Main Buddha Hall.

Anna: It looks so real!

Seunim: Now, it's your turn.

Keep your paper cup standing straight.

Place some glue on the bottom of the flower petal. Glue them on the edge of the paper cup in a single row.

Anna: I completed the first row after gluing five flower petals.

Seunim: Good. Now, continue with gluing the second and third rows.

Anna: I need to be very careful.

The petals are very delicate.

마음달이 외로이 둥글어

마음달이 외로이 둥글어
그 빛이 만상을 삼켰네
빛과 경계를 함께 잊으면
다시 이것이 무엇인고

_경허 선사

The light of the lonely mind of the full moon

The light of the lonely mind of the full moon
Has engulfed all things;
When both light and object are forgotten
What is this again?

_By Ven. Gyeongheo

6 경전 탁본

애나: 이 탁본은 정말 멋지네요.

잭: 글만이 아니라 그림도 있어 좋아요.

애나: 이제 당신 차례예요. 한번 해보세요.

잭: 좋아요. 먼저 경판에 먹물을 바르고…

스님: 먹물을 고루 묻혀야 된답니다.

잭: 네, 스님! 이제 한지를 대고 잘 문지르면 되지요?

스님: 맞아요. 그렇게 꾹꾹 잘 눌러서 문지르면 됩니다. 작품이 잘 나왔네요.

애나: 스님, 이 한지는 제가 평소 쓰던 종이와 다르네요.

스님: 네, 닥나무로 만든 한국의 전통 종이랍니다.

Unit 6 ## Rubbing a Sutra

Anna: This rubbing of a sutra is wonderful.

Jack: I like it because it has both script and illustrations.

Anna: It's your turn. Give it a try.

Jack: Ok, so you have to brush ink on the woodblock…

Seunim: Make sure you evenly brush on the ink.

Jack: Yes, Seunim! Now I should place the hanji on and rub it?

Seunim: Yes, just as you are doing. Make sure you rub and press the paper well. It looks great!

Anna: Seunim, this hanji is different from the paper I use every day.

Seunim: It is traditional Korean paper made from paper mulberry trees.

○ ~을 한번 해보세요, 시도해보세요   **Give it a try**

○ ~을 반드시 하세요   **Make sure to** 동사
이 단어들을 반드시 외우세요. Make sure to memorize the words.
문을 반드시 닫으세요. Make sure to close the door.
설명서를 반드시 읽으세요. Make sure to read the instructions.
신발을 반드시 벗으세요. Make sure to take off your shoes.

○ ~을 하는 것처럼   **Just as you are** '동사 + **ing** (동명사)'
당신이 자르고 있는 것처럼. Just as you are cutting.
당신이 노래하고 있는 것처럼. Just as you are singing.
당신이 그리고 있는 것처럼. Just as you are drawing.

○ 닥나무   **paper mulberry tree**
한지는 닥나무 속껍질로 만든다.
Hanji is made from the inner bark of the paper mulberry tree, or daknamu.

○ 한지   **hanji**
그녀는 불교와 한지의 역사적 관계를 연구했다.
She researched historical connections between Buddhism and hanji.
한국의 수제 한지는 한약(허브)을 보관하는 데 좋다.
Handmade Korean paper, called hanji, is an excellent material for storing herbs.

○ 칭찬   **Compliment**
아주 잘했습니다! You did great!
매우 훌륭해 보입니다! It looks wonderful!
정말 잘했습니다! What a great job!
뛰어난 실력입니다. This is outstanding!

○ 국보   **(Korean) National Treasure**

Pair Work

Anna: This rubbing of a sutra is <u>spectacular</u>.
Jack: I like it because it has both <u>words and pictures</u>.
Anna: <u>You are next</u>. Give it a try.
Seunim: <u>Try to</u> evenly brush on the ink.
Jack: Yes, Seunim! Now <u>can I put</u> the hanji on and rub it?
Seunim: Yes. <u>You are doing a great job</u>. Make sure you rub
and press the paper well. It looks great!

1 법당의 불보살

스님: 여기가 석가모니 부처님을 모신 대웅전입니다.

잭: 그런데 불단에 부처님이 왜 이렇게 많아요?

스님: 보통 본존을 좌우에서 모시는 협시불이 있습니다.

잭: 일종의 수행원인가요?

스님: 그렇다고 할 수 있지요. 석가모니 부처님의 경우
　　　보통 문수보살과 보현보살이 좌우에서 모십니다.

잭: 제가 여러 절을 방문하면서 늘 궁금하던 것이 있어요.

스님: 말씀해보세요.

잭: 절에 가면 왜 그렇게 부처님과 보살님의 상이 많은가요?

스님: 이 우주에는 곳곳에 무수히 많은 부처와 보살이 계신답니다.
　　　중생의 능력과 수준이 다 다르기 때문에 근기에 맞는 가르침을 펴주시지요.

Unit 1 ## Buddhas and Bodhisattva at the Main Buddha Hall

Seunim: This is the Main Buddha Hall where we enshrine the
　　　　　Sakyamuni Buddha.

Jack: Why are there so many buddha statues on the altar?

Seunim: Generally, there are attendant buddhas or bodhisattvas on both
　　　　　sides of the main Buddha.

Jack: Are they some type of Buddha entourage?

Seunim: Yes, you can say that. Usually for Sakyamuni Buddha,
　　　　　Munsubosal or Manjusri Bodhisattva is placed on the left, and
　　　　　Bohyeonbosal or Samantabhadra bodhisattva stands on the right
　　　　　side.

Jack: I've always wondered about something whenever I visit a temple.

Seunim: What is that?

Jack: Why are there so many buddha and bodhisattva statues in temples?

Seunim: In this universe, there are many buddhas and bodhisattvas. They always teach sentient beings according to each sentient being's own capabilities.

Words and Phrases

○ 왜 ~가 많지요?　**Why are there so many** 명사 **?**
　왜 이곳에는 사람이 많지요?　Why are there so many people here?
　왜 이 공원에는 꽃이 많이 피었지요?　Why are there so many flowers in the park?

○ 일반적으로, 대체로　**generally**
　일반적으로 저희는 예약만 받습니다.　Generally, we only accept reservations.
　대체로 학생들은 저희 책을 좋아합니다.　Generally, students like our books.

○ ~종류의, 모종의　**Some type of** 명사
　모종의 공연을 하고 있어요.　They are having some type of performance.
　그것은 약의 종류입니다.　That is some type of medicine.

○ 중생　**sentient beings**
○ 대웅전　**Main Buddha Hall**
○ 석가모니 부처님　**Sakyamuni Buddha**
○ 문수보살　**Manjusri**
○ 보현보살　**Samantabhadra**

○ 많은, 여러 가지의　**many** + 가산명사
　여러 가지 수행 방법이 있습니다.　There are many ways to practice.
　오늘 많은 불자들이 모였습니다.　Many Buddhists gathered today.
　이 요리엔 많은 재료들이 들어갑니다.　Many ingredients go in this dish.

Seunim: <u>Here we are at the</u> Main Buddha Hall where we enshrine the Sakyamuni Buddha.

Jack: <u>Is there a reason why several</u> buddha statues are on the altar?

Seunim: <u>It's because we have</u> an attendant buddha or bodhisattva on both sides of the Main Buddha.

Jack: <u>Can we call them</u> Buddha's entourage?

Seunim: Yes, <u>you got it</u>. For Sakyamuni Buddha, usually, Munsubosal or Manjusri Bodhisattva stands on the left and Bohyeonbosal or Samantabhadra stands on the right side.

Jack: <u>I was always curious</u> about something after visiting many temples.

Seunim: <u>Can you tell me more</u>?

Jack: <u>Is there a meaning behind having</u> so many buddha and bodhisattva statues in temples?

Seunim: <u>There are many buddhas and bodhisattvas in this universe</u>. They always teach sentient beings according to each sentient being's own capabilities and tolerances.

찬불가 1

보현행원

내 이제 두 손 모아 청하옵나니
시방세계 부처님 우주대광명
두 눈 어둔 이 내 몸 굽어살피사
위없는 대법문을 널리 여소서
허공계와 중생계가 다할지라도
오늘 세운 이 서원은 끝없사오리

_작사 정운문

Buddhist Hymns 1

The Vows of Samantabhadra

I now supplicate with joined palms
Let the great light of all buddhas in the ten directions
Look over me who is blinded by ignorance
And spread the unsurpassed teachings far and wide
Even if the realms of space and sentient beings end
The vows I have made today will not end

_Lyrics by Jeong Un-mun

② 산사

스님: 애나! 산사에 와보니 어때요?

애나: 정말 좋아요.

그런데 한국 절은 왜 주로 산중에 있는지요?

스님: 우선 한국인들이 산을 좋아하고 한국에는 산이 많기 때문이지요.

애나: 저도 산에 오면 좋은 기운을 느껴요.

스님: 그리고 인적이 드물어 수도에 도움이 됩니다.

애나: 그렇겠네요.

스님: 그리고 조선시대에 불교를 억압한 정책의 영향도 있지요.

애나: 그렇군요. 그래도 저는 절이 산에 있는 게 참 좋아요.

Unit 2 ## Temple in the Mountain

Seunim: Anna! What do you think about this temple in the mountains?

Anna: I love it. Why are many of the Korean Buddhist temples located in the mountains?

Seunim: It's because Koreans love mountains and geographically, there are many mountains in Korea.

Anna: I can feel good energy when I come to the mountains.

Seunim: Also, because there aren't many people around, it is very helpful for our practice.

Anna: I can see why.

Seunim: Another reason is because of the suppression of Buddhism during the Joseon Dynasty.

Anna: I see. I really love the temples in the mountains.

○ ~에 대해 어떻게 생각하세요? ~는 어떤가요?   **What do you think about ~ 명사?**
이 드레스는 어떤가요?   What do you think about this dress?
이 카메라는 어떤가요?   What do you think about this camera?
이 여행에 대해 어떻게 생각하세요?   What do you think about this trip?

○ ~하면 ~한 기분이에요   **I feel + 형용사 when I + 동사**
운동을 하면 기운이 나요.   I feel energized when I exercise.
템플스테이에 참여하면 평화로운 기분이 들어요.   I feel peaceful when I participate in a Templestay.
친구들과 어울리면 기분이 좋아져요.   I feel great when I hang out with my friends.

○ 억압   **suppression**

○ 이유를 알 수 있다   **Can see why**
왜 이 사찰이 유명한지 아시겠어요?   Can you see why this temple is so famous?
주의사항을 지켜야 하는 이유를 알겠습니다.   I can see why I have to follow the rules.

○ 진짜로, 정말   **Really** (부사)
정말로 어떻게 생각하세요?   What do you really think?
배가 진짜 고파요.   I am really hungry.

○ 등산   **Mountain climbing, hiking** (본격적인 등반은 **mountain climbing**, 그보다 가벼운 등산은 **hiking**임)
저의 취미는 등산입니다.   My hobby is hiking.
등산을 하면 몸에 좋습니다.   Hiking is good for your health.

Pair Work

Seunim: Anna, how do you feel about visiting the temple in the mountains?

Anna: I love it. I was wondering about why so many Korean Buddhist temples are located in the mountains.

Seunim: It's because of Koreans' love for the mountains. Also, Korea is very mountainous.

Anna: Mountains give me good energy.

Seunim: Also, because it's not very populated here, it is very helpful for our practice.

Anna: I see your point.

Seunim: In addition, there was a suppression of Buddhism during the Joseon Dynasty.

Anna: I see. I really treasure the temples in the mountains.

③ 대중생활

잭: 스님, 절에 스님들이 몇 분이나 계시나요?

스님: 일곱 분입니다.

잭: 스님들은 원래 이렇게 모여 사시나요?

스님: '승가'라는 말이 공동체를 이루고 살아가는 대중을 의미합니다.

잭: 저는 혼자 사는 것이 편하던데요.

스님: 함께 살면서 서로 양보하고 배려하여 화합하는 법을 배운답니다.
덧붙여 계율을 잘 지키는 법도 익힐 수 있고요.

Unit 3 Communal Life

Jack: Seunim, how many seunims are here at the temple?

Seunim: There are seven of us.

Jack: Do seunims normally live together like this?

Seunim: Sangha means a monastic community that lives a communal life.

Jack: Personally, I think living alone is more comfortable.

Seunim: We learn how to live harmoniously by being considerate to others and putting other people before ourselves. Also, we can learn how to observe and follow the precepts.

○ ~ 있습니다   **There are** + 명사
몇 백 그루의 나무가 있습니다.   There are hundreds of trees.
이천 권의 책이 있어요.   There are two thousand books.
15명의 참가자가 있어요.   There are fifteen participants.

○ 원래 이렇게 합니다   **Normally,** (명사 + 동사) **like this**
우리는 원래 이렇게 일합니다.   Normally, we work like this.
우리는 원래 이렇게 수행합니다.   Normally, we practice like this.

○ ~을 따르다, 지키다   **follow** + 명사
지시 사항을 따르다.   Follow the instructions.
규정을 지키다.   Follow the regulations.

○ 편하다   **comfortable**
사찰에 머무는 것이 편하게 느껴진다.   I feel comfortable staying at a temple.
방석에 앉는 것이 편한가요?   Do you feel comfortable sitting on a cushion?
그것에 대해 논하는 것이 불편합니다 (거절의 의사).   I don't feel comfortable sharing that information.

○ 편리하다   **Convenient**
이메일로 소식을 주고받으니 매우 편리합니다.   It is very convenient to communicate through email.
편리하시도록 이메일을 보내 드리겠습니다.   For your convenience, I will send you an email.

Pair Work

Jack: Seunim, <u>in this temple, how many seunims live here?</u>

Seunim: <u>We have seven seunims here</u>.

Jack: <u>Is it a common practice for</u> seunims to live together?

Seunim: Sangha means a <u>congregation of people living as a</u> community.

Jack: <u>For me</u>, I think living alone is more <u>convenient</u>.

Seunim: We learn how to live harmoniously by being considerate to others and putting other people before ourselves. Also, <u>we learn and teach others how to</u> follow the Buddhist rules.

4 일주문의 의미

애나: 스님! 일주문은 어디에 있어요?

스님: 애나가 절에 들어올 때 처음 들어온 문을 말해요.

애나: 그럼 기둥이 하나밖에 없나요?

스님: 기둥이 일직선상의 한 줄로 있다고 해서 일주문이에요.

애나: 아, 이제 기억이 나요.

스님: 그 문을 들어설 때 마음이 하나가 되어야 한다는 의미도 있어요.

애나: 아이쿠, 저는 남자친구 생각을 하면서 들어왔는데...
　　　 나갔다가 다시 들어와야겠네요.

Unit 4 ## The One Pillar Gate

Anna: Seunim! Where is the One Pillar Gate?

Seunim: It's the first gate that you entered through when you came into the temple.

Anna: Does it have only one column?

Seunim: The One Pillar Gate was named after the fact that its pillars are lined up in one straight line.

Anna: Yes, I do remember now.

Seunim: It also means your mind should become "one" when you enter through this gate.

Anna: Oops, I was thinking about my boyfriend when I walked in. I should go back and enter again.

○ ~하다는 뜻인가요?　**Does it mean** + 주어 + 동사?
우리에겐 두 시간밖에 없다는 뜻인가요?　Does it mean we only have two hours?
그는 떠나야 한다는 뜻인가요?　Does it mean he has to leave?
그녀가 다시 해야만 한다는 뜻인가요?　Does it mean she has to do it again?

○ ~의 이름을 따라 짓다　주어 + **was named after** + 명사
그의 이름은 아버지의 이름을 따라 지어졌다.　He was named after his father.
이곳은 내려오는 전설에서 명명되었다.　This place was named after the legend.

○ 기억하다, 유념하다　**remember**
그 일을 기억하십니까?　Do you remember that event?
제가 보내드린 서류 기억하세요?　Do you remember the form that I sent you?
여권 가져오는 걸 기억하시기 바랍니다.　Please remember to bring your passport.

○ 돌아가다　**go back**
맨 처음으로 돌아가 다시 읽어보세요.　Go back to the beginning and read it again.
다시 집으로 돌아가야겠어요.　I have to go back home.

Pair Work

Anna: Seunim! <u>Can you point to</u> where the One Pillar Gate is <u>at?</u>

Seunim: It's the first gate that you <u>came through</u> when you <u>entered</u> the temple.

Anna: Does it mean <u>there's only</u> one column?

Seunim: The One Pillar Gate was <u>named after the fact that</u> both columns are in alignment.

Anna: Yes, <u>I get it now</u>.

Seunim: It also <u>teaches you that</u> your mind should become "one" when you enter the temple.

Anna: Oops, I was thinking about my boyfriend when I walked in. I should leave and <u>come through the gate again</u>.

5 사찰생활의 자연보존

스님: 잭은 환경운동을 한다고 했지요?

잭: 네, 10년째 하고 있습니다.

스님: 환경운동가가 본 사찰생활은 어떤가요?

잭: 매우 환경친화적이지요.

스님: 어떤 면에서 그런가요?

잭: 우선 식생활에서 버리는 음식이 없어요.

스님: 그래요. (스님들은) 쌀 한 톨도 귀하게 여기지요. 시주의 은혜에 대한 고마움을 늘 지니고 생활하지요. 옛 스님께서는 쌀 한 톨의 시주 무게가 7근이라고도 하셨답니다.

잭: 채식도 환경보존에 일조하고요. 특히 채식은 '불살생'이라는 불교의 계율이 적용되어 생명존중의 사상과도 연결되고 있습니다.

스님: 그러고 보니 스님들의 의생활도 환경보존에 기여한답니다.

잭: 어째서요?

스님: 저는 옷이 3벌밖에 없거든요. 하하하…

Unit 5 Monastic Life Preserves Nature

Seunim: Jack, you said you are involved in the environmental movement?

Jack: Yes, I've been doing it for 10 years.

Seunim: How is monastic life from an environmentalist's perspective?

Jack: It's very environmentally friendly.

Seunim: In what area?

Jack: First, there is no food waste.

Seunim: Yes, we treasure even a single grain of rice. We have always lived with gratitude for our patrons in mind. Old seunims from the past said a single grain of rice equals 7 pounds of a patron's good deeds.

Jack: Being vegetarian also contributes to preserving the environment. In particular, vegetarianism embodies the Buddhist precept "Refrain from killing" and thus, is directly connected with the Buddhist philosophy of respect for life.

Seunim: Come to think of it, a seunim's clothing helps preserve the environment, too.

Jack: How so?

Seunim: Because I only own three sets of clothes. Hahaha…

Words and Phrases

○ ~동안 하고 있다 **I've been** + 동사 **+ ing** (동명사)
2년 동안 참선을 수행하고 있다. I've been practicing meditation for two years.
3년 동안 영어를 공부하고 있다. I've been studying English for three years.

○ ~의 관점에서 **From** + 소유격 명사 **(or** 형용사**)** + **perspective**
나의 관점에서. From my perspective ~.
불자의 관점에서. From a Buddhist's perspective ~.
동양의 관점에서. From the Eastern perspective ~.

○ ~에 친화적이다 **It's very** + 명사 + **friendly**
애완동물에 친화적이다. It's very pet friendly.
가족끼리 방문하기에 좋은 장소이다. It's a very family friendly place to visit.

○ ~에 일조하다, ~에 기여하다 **Contribute to**
나는 그의 캠페인에 일조했다. I contributed to his campaign.
나라를 위해 기여할 수 있는 것이 무엇일까요? What can you contribute to the country?

○ 생각해보니~ **Come to think of it~**
생각해보니 저는 언제나 불교에 관심이 있었어요. Come to think of it, I always had an interest in Buddhism.
생각해보니 당신이 그 일에 적임자겠군요! Come to think of it, you will be a great person for that job.

○ 부분, 분야, 영역 **area**
어떤 분야에서 일하시나요? What area of industry do you work in?
어떤 부분이 우려되시나요? In what area do you have a concern for?

○ 시주자   **patron, supporter**
시주   donation, offering
시주를 하다.   make a donation, make an offering
기와 한 장 시주하세요.   Please donate a roof tile for the temple.
쌀 한 톨의 무게가 일곱 근(一米七斤).
Old seunims from the past said a single grain of rice equals 7 pounds of a patron's good deeds.
(여기서는 시주의 은혜가 그리 무겁다는 말이므로 굳이 7근을 9파운드나 3.5킬로그램으로 번역할 필요는 없다.)

○ 소유, 보유하다   **own**
나는 매우 아름다운 집을 가지고 있습니다.   I own a beautiful house.
그녀는 큰 농장을 소유하고 있습니다.   She owns a large farm.
그가 이 산의 소유주입니다.   He is the owner of this mountain.

Pair Work

Seunim: Jack, you <u>had mentioned that you</u> are involved in the environmental movement?

Jack: Yes, for 10 years.

Seunim: How is monastic life from an environmentalist's <u>eyes</u>?

Jack: It's very environmentally <u>conscious</u>.

Seunim: In what <u>perspective</u>?

Jack: First, there <u>aren't any food leftovers</u>.

Seunim: Yes, we treasure <u>everything we eat</u>. We have always lived with <u>thankfulness</u> for our <u>supporters</u> in mind. Old seunims from the past said a single grain of rice equals 7 pounds of a patron's good deeds.

Jack: Being vegetarian also <u>helps in</u> preserving the environment.

Seunim: Come to think of it, a seunim's clothing helps <u>protect</u> the environment, too.

Jack: <u>In what ways</u>?

Seunim: Because I only <u>have</u> three sets of clothes. Hahaha…

산회가

몸은 비록 이 자리에서 헤어지지만
마음은 언제라도 떠나지 마세
거룩하신 부처님 항상 모시고
오늘 배운 높은 법문 깊이 새겨서
다음 날 반갑게 한 맘 한 뜻으로
부처님의 성전에 다시 만나세.

_작사 정운문

Buddhist Hymns 2

Song of Adjournment

Though we part in our bodies
Let us not part in our minds
Always dwelling in the presence of the Buddha
Engraving today's sublime teaching in our hearts
Let us be reunited joyfully at the next gathering
With one mind in the sacred hall of the Buddha

_Lyrics by Jeong Un-mun

지대방
이야기

6 연꽃의 의미

잭: 스님! 연꽃과 불교는 무슨 관계가 있나요?

스님: 연꽃은 아름다운 꽃을 피우죠.
그런데 그 뿌리와 줄기를 보면 어디에서 자라지요?

애나: 연못이나 호수요.

스님: 그 연못이나 호수 물이 맑던가요?

애나: 아니요, 탁하고 지저분해요.

스님: 네. 그런 더러운 물속 진흙에서 연꽃은 핀답니다.
또 연꽃은 높은 곳이 아닌 낮은 지대에서 자라고, 연꽃과 잎은 물에 젖지 않는 성질을 지니고 있지요. 그리고 꽃과 열매가 동시에 열리기에 "초발심시변정각"이라는 구절로도 표현하기도 하지요. 그러니 번뇌로 가득한 세상에서 그것에 물들지 않고 연꽃처럼 맑고 아름다운 마음으로 살라는 의미입니다.

Unit 6 The Meaning of the Lotus Flower

Jack: Seunim, what is the relationship between the lotus flower and Buddhism?

Seunim: Lotus flowers bloom beautifully.

However, if you look at its stems and roots, where do they grow?

Anna: In a pond or lake.

Seunim: If you look closely, do those ponds and lakes have clear water?

Anna: No, usually they are very muddy and dirty.

Seunim: Yes, a lotus flower blooms from muddy and dirty water. They grow in low places and the leaves are water repellent. Also, because lotus plants bear fruits and flowers at the same time, we say "Chobalsimsi Byeonjeonggak," which means "the very first moment of aspiration for enlightenment itself is the moment of true awakening." It means to live with a pure and beautiful mind like a lotus flower instead of being influenced by the world filled with afflictions.

Words and Phrases

○ ~은 무슨 관계인가요?　**Relationship between ~ 명사 and 명사**
　참선과 수행은 어떤 관계가 있나요?　What is the relationship between meditation and practice?
　이 지도와 우리의 여행은 무슨 관계가 있나요?　What is the relationship between this map and our trip?

○ 자세히 보면　**If you look closely**
　자세히 보면 그림의 특징이 보입니다.　If you look closely, you can see the picture's character.
　자세히 보면 숨은 의미가 보입니다.　If you look closely, you can see the hidden meanings.

○ 깨달음　**enlightenment**

○ 번뇌　**afflictions, defilements**

○ 관점, 시각　**perspective, point of view**
　사람은 각자의 관점을 가지고 있다.　People have their own perspectives.
　모든 사람들의 관점을 들어보도록 하죠.　Let's hear everyone's point of view.

○ 성장, 자라다　**grow**
　한국 경제는 빠르게 성장했다.　The Korean economy grew fast.
　그는 지혜로운 사람으로 성장했다.　He grew up to be a wise person.

○ 눈깜빡할 사이에　**(in the) blink of an eye**
　한 해가 눈깜빡할 사이에 지났다.　This year has passed in the blink of an eye.
　하루가 눈깜빡할 사이에 지나갈 겁니다.　The day will pass in the blink of an eye.

Seunim: If you look <u>carefully</u>, do those ponds and lakes have <u>clean</u> water?

Anna: No, <u>generally</u>, they are very muddy and dirty.

Seunim: Yes, a lotus flower <u>grows in</u> muddy and dirty water. They bloom in lower regions and the leaves have a water <u>resistant</u> nature. Also, because lotus plants bear fruits and flowers at the same time, we say "Chobalsimsi Byeonjeonggak," which means "the moment one begins to aspire for enlightenment itself is the true awakening." It <u>teaches us</u> to live with a pure and beautiful mind like the lotus flower instead of being influenced by the world filled with afflictions.

청산은 나를 보고

청산은 나를 보고 말 없이 살라 하고
창공은 나를 보고 티 없이 살라 하네
성냄도 벗어 놓고 탐욕도 벗어 놓고
물처럼 바람처럼 살다가 가라 하네.

_나옹 선사

Blue Mountain Tells Me

Blue mountain tells me to live in silence
Blue sky tells me to live in purity
To let go of anger and to let go of greed
To live like the water and to live like the wind

_By Ven. Naong

1 사찰 위치 문의

(사찰의 위치를 문의하는 전화가 온다.)

스님: 여보세요.

애나: 여보세요, 거기가 조계사인가요?

스님: 예, 그렇습니다.

애나: 제가 거기로 찾아가려고 합니다.

위치가 어떻게 되나요?

스님: 조계사는 서울 시내에 있습니다.

지하철 안국역에서 6번 출구로 나오시면 됩니다.

애나: 주변에 큰 건물이 있습니까?

스님: 네. '템플스테이 홍보관'이라는 건물이 있는데, 그 맞은편에 조계사가 있습니다.

주변으로 한국 전통문화 거리인 인사동과 북촌이 있답니다.

Unit 1 **An Inquiry about the Temple Location**

(Receiving a phone call asking for the temple's location)

Seunim: Hello?

Anna: Hello, is this Jogye-sa?

Seunim: Yes, it is.

Anna: I would like to get to your temple. Where are you located at?

Seunim: Jogye-sa is located in downtown Seoul. You may exit through exit number 6 at the Anguk subway station.

Anna: Are there any big buildings nearby?

Seunim: We are located across the street from the Templestay Information Center. The streets of Insa-dong and Bukchon, which are centers of Korean traditional culture, are within walking distance from us.

Words and Phrases

○ ～인가요?　**Is this** + 명사? (전화로 통화할 때)
쌍계사인가요?　Is this Ssangyesa?
제임스인가요?　Is this James?

○ ～에 가고 싶습니다　**I would like to get to** + 명사
제 호텔에 가고 싶습니다.　I would like to get to my hotel.
명동에 가고 싶습니다.　I would like to get to Myeongdong.
부산에 가고 싶습니다.　I would like to get to Busan.
제주도에 가고 싶습니다.　I would like to get to Jejudo.

○ ～은 어디에 있습니까?　**Where is** + 명사 + **located at?**
백화점은 어디에 있습니까?　Where is the department store located at?
경찰서는 어디에 있습니까?　Where is the police station located at?
화장실은 어디에 있습니까?　Where is the bathroom located at?
우체국은 어디에 있습니까?　Where is the post office located at?

○ ～은 ～에 위치하고 있습니다　명사 + **is located at ～**
할머니 댁은 123길에 있습니다.　My grandmother's house is located on 123rd Street.
저희 가게는 오른편에 있습니다.　Our store is located on the right side.
도서관은 파란 빌딩 옆에 있습니다.　The library is located next to a blue building.
식당은 슈퍼마켓 뒤에 있습니다.　The restaurant is located behind the grocery store.

○ 슈퍼마켓　**grocery store** (supermarket은 미국에서는 자주 쓰이지 않는 표현)

○ 지나치고, 너무 멀리 가다　**missed it and went too far**
ABC길이 보이면 우리 사찰을 지나치고 너무 멀리 가신 겁니다.
If you see ABC Street, you missed our temple and went too far.

○ ～쪽으로 가다　**Turn ～**
파란 간판이 보이면 오른쪽으로 가세요.　Turn right when you see a blue sign.

○ 신호등　**traffic light**

47

Seunim: Hello?

Anna: Hello, is this Jogyesa?

Seunim: Yes, <u>it is</u>.

Anna: I would like to <u>visit</u> your temple. <u>Can you tell me your location?</u>

Seunim: Jogye-sa is located in downtown Seoul. We are <u>next to</u> Insa-dong.

Anna: Are there any <u>landmarks</u> nearby?

Seunim: <u>You can find us at</u> the intersection of Anguk-dong. Pungmun Girl's High School and Jongro Police Station are <u>very close to us</u>.

찬불가 4

청법가

덕 높으신 스승님 사자좌에 오르사
사자후를 합소서 감로법을 주소서
옛 인연을 잇도록 새 인연을 맺도록
대자비를 베푸사 법을 설하옵소서

_작사 이광수

Buddhist Hymns 4

Request of a Teaching

Virtuous teacher! Please mount the lion's throne
And utter a lion's roar. Bestow upon us ambrosial Dharma!
To be able to let go of old ties and make new ties
We request you to teach us with your great compassion

_Lyrics by Yi Gwang-su

② 사찰 교통편 문의

(사찰 위치 문의 전화가 교통편 문의로 이어진다.)

애나: 스님, 죄송하지만 교통편을 좀 알려주세요.

스님: 지금 계신 곳이 어디인지요?

애나: 저는 약수역 근처에 있습니다.

스님: 그럼 3호선을 타고 오십시오.
지도에 오렌지색으로 표시가 되어 있습니다.

애나: 예, 찾았어요.

스님: 약수역에서 3호선 대화행을 타십시오.
그리고 안국역 6번 출구로 나오세요.
거기서 도보로 3분 정도면 조계사에 도착합니다.

애나: 감사합니다.

Unit 2   An Inquiry on Transportation to the Temple

(A location inquiry leads to questions on transportation.)

Anna: Seunim, would you mind telling me how to get to the temple?

Seunim: Where are you located right now?

Anna: I am near Yaksu Station.

Seunim: You can take the subway line 3. It's marked in orange.

Anna: Yes, I found it.

Seunim: From Yaksu Station, take line 3 towards Daehwa. Get off at Anguk Station and exit through exit number 6. You will walk about three minutes before you arrive at Jogye-sa.

Anna: Thank you.

○ 죄송하지만 ~할 수 있을까요? (정중한 부탁)　**Would you mind 동사 + ing?**
죄송하지만 소금 좀 주시겠습니까?　Would you mind passing me the salt?
죄송하지만 다시 말씀해주시겠습니까?　Would you mind repeating that?

○ ~을 찾았어요　**I found + 명사**
답을 찾았어요.　I found the answer.
식당을 찾았어요.　I found the restaurant.
도서관을 찾았어요.　I found the library.

○ ~근처에 있습니다　**I am near + 명사**
인사동 근처에 있습니다.　I am near Insa-dong.
정문 근처에 있습니다.　I am near the front gate.
분수대 근처에 있습니다.　I am near the fountain.

○ ~을 타다　**Get on + 명사**
버스를 타다.　Get on the bus.
전철을 타다.　Get on the subway.
비행기를 타다.　Get on the airplane.

○ ~에서 내리다　**Get off +명사**
기차에서 내리다.　Get off the train

○ ~정도 걸립니다　**It will take about**
도보로 10분 정도 걸립니다.　It will take about ten minutes on foot.
차로 20분 정도 걸립니다.　It will take about twenty minutes by car.

○ 잠시 후에 뵙겠습니다　**See you soon**

○ 만나 뵐 수 있기를 기대하겠습니다　**I look forward to meeting you**

Pair Work

Anna: Seunim, would you be so kind to tell me how to get to the temple?

Seunim: Where are you departing from?

Anna: I am close to Yaksu Station.

Seunim: You can get on subway line 3. It's the orange line.

Anna: Yes, I see it.

Seunim: At Yaksu Station, take line 3 towards Daehwa. Get off at Anguk Station and come out through exit number 6. After walking about three minutes you will see Jogye-sa.

③ 스님과의 통화

(한국에 체류 중인 잭이 전화로 선재 스님을 찾는다.)

스님: 여보세요.

잭: 여보세요? 거기가 대각사입니까?

스님: 예, 그렇습니다.

잭: 선재 스님과 통화를 할 수 있을까요?

스님: 예, 누구시라고 전할까요?

잭: 미국에서 온 잭입니다.

스님: 잠깐만 기다리세요. (잠시 후) 미안하지만 지금 안 계시네요.

잭: 저 그럼 전화 부탁드린다고 전해주세요.

　　　제 핸드폰 번호는 010-2154-1551입니다.

스님: 네, 전해드리지요.

Unit 3 ## Having a Phone Conversation with a Seunim

(Jack, who is staying in Korea, is looking for Seonjae Seunim over the phone)

Seunim: Hello.

Jack:　Hello? Is this Daegak-sa?

Seunim: Yes, it is.

Jack:　May I speak with Seonjae Seunim?

Seunim: Sure. May I ask who is calling?

Jack:　This is Jack from the USA.

Seunim: One moment please.

　　　　　(moments later) I am sorry but Seonjae Seunim is out at the

　　　　　moment.

Jack: Would you have Seonjae Seunim give me a call? My mobile number is zero one zero, two one five four, one five five one.

Seunim: Sure, I will deliver your message.

○ 해인사입니다. 무엇을 도와드릴까요?　**This is Haein-sa. How may I help you?**

○ (전화상으로) 네, 접니다　(남자일 경우) **This is he** / (여자일 경우) **This is she**

○ 담당자를 바꿔 드리겠습니다　**Let me transfer you to the person who is in charge**

○ 담당자가 자리를 비우셨네요　**The person in charge is away from the desk**

○ 제가 도와드리고 싶지만 아쉽게도 필요하신 것에 대한 정보를 가지고 있지 않습니다.
I would like to help, but I do not have the information you need.

○ 메시지를 꼭 전달해 드리겠습니다　**I will make sure to deliver your message**

○ 한 시간 뒤에 전화하시면 담당자와 통화하실 수 있습니다.
If you call back in one hour, you can speak to the person in charge.

○ 다시 전화할 때 현공 스님을 찾으세요　**When you call back, ask for Hyeongong Seunim**

○ ～에서 온 ～입니다 (전화 통화일 때)　**This is** + 명사 **from** + 명사
뉴욕에서 온 시원입니다.　This is Siwon from New York.
멕시코에서 온 마리아입니다.　This is Maria from Mexico.
서울에서 온 수아입니다.　This is Sooa from Seoul.

○ ～가 ～을 하게 해주시겠습니까?　**Would you have** + 명사 + 동사?
어머니께 내게 전화해 달라고 전해주시겠어요?　Would you have your mom give me a call?
프런트데스크에 5시에 제게 전화하라고 해주시겠어요?　Would you have the front desk call me at five?
탐한테 제게 편지해 달라고 해주시겠어요?　Would you have Tom send me a letter?

Jack: <u>I am looking for</u> Seonjae Seunim?

Seunim: Sure. May I ask <u>who this is</u>?

Jack: <u>I am</u> Jack from the USA.

Seunim: <u>Let me place you on hold</u>.

(moments later…) I am sorry but Seonjae Seunim <u>is away at this time</u>.

Jack: Would you <u>tell</u> Seonjae Seunim to give me a call? My mobile number is zero one zero, two one five four, one five five one.

Seunim: Sure, I will <u>convey</u> your message.

찬불가 3

우리도 부처님같이

어둠은 한순간 그대로가 빛이라네
바른 생각 바른말 바른 행동이
무명을 거두고 우주를 밝히는
이제는 가슴 깊이 깨달을 수 있다네
정진하세 정진하세 물러남이 없는 정진
우리도 부처님같이 우리도 부처님같이

_작사 맹석분

Buddhist Hymns 3

Let us Emulate the Buddha

Darkness is light as it is though it may last momentarily
Right thought, right speech and right action
Extinguish ignorance and illuminate the universe
Now we realize in the depth of our hearts
Let us practice diligently without any regression
Let us emulate the Buddha, emulate the Buddha

_Lyrics by Maeng Seonk-bun

템플스테이 문의 전화

스님: 예, 범어사입니다.

애나: 저, 그곳에서 외국인 템플스테이를 운영하는가요?

스님: 예, 합니다.

애나: 그럼 이번 주말에 참가할 수 있을까요?

스님: 이번 주말은 이미 예약이 끝났습니다.

애나: 그럼 다음 주말은 가능한가요?

스님: 가능합니다. 예약을 해드릴까요?

애나: 아닙니다. 제가 직접 인터넷으로 예약을 하고 신청비도 지불하겠습니다.

스님: 예, 그럼 다음 주 토요일에 뵙겠습니다.

애나: 감사합니다.

Unit 4 ## A Phone Inquiry about Templestay

Seunim: This is Beomeo-sa.

Anna: Hello, do you offer a Templestay for foreigners?

Seunim: Yes, we do.

Anna: Would it be possible to participate this weekend?

Seunim: Unfortunately, all reservations for this weekend are booked.

Anna: Would next weekend be possible?

Seunim: Yes, would you like to make a reservation?

Anna: No, I will register on-line and make the reservation myself.

Seunim: OK, we will see you next Saturday then.

Anna: Thank you.

○ ~을 할 수 있을까요?　**Would it be possible to** + 동사?

　내일부터 시작할 수 있을까요?　Would it be possible to start tomorrow?

　다음 주 토요일부터 동참할 수 있을까요?　Would it be possible to join next Saturday?

　한 가지 요청을 할 수 있을까요?　Would it be possible to make a request?

○ 다 찼습니다　**All booked (up)**

○ ~언제 뵙겠습니다　**See you** + 날짜

　다음 주 토요일에 뵙겠습니다.　See you next Saturday.

　내일 뵙겠습니다.　See you tomorrow.

　2주 후에 뵙겠습니다.　See you in two weeks.

　다음 주 목요일에 뵙겠습니다.　See you on the following Thursday.

○ 템플스테이에 혼자 참가하시나요?　**Are you coming to the Templestay by yourself?**

○ 다른 일행이 있으신가요?　**Will you come with other parties?**

○ 모두 몇 분이 템플스테이에 참가하고 싶으신가요?

　How many of you would like to participate in the Templestay?

○ 두 자리밖에 남아 있지 않네요　**There are only two more availabilities.**

○ 참가 기한에 여유가 있으신가요?　**Are you flexible on your dates? (or) Are your dates flexible?**

○ 이메일 주소를 주시면 자세한 사항을 보내 드리겠습니다.

　If you give me your email address, I will send you some detailed information.

○ 참가비는 하루에 5만 원입니다　**The participating fee is fifty thousand Korean Won per day.**

○ 질문이 있으면 언제든지 연락하세요　**If you have any questions, please call us anytime.**

Pair Work

Anna:　Hello, do you <u>have</u> a Templestay for foreigners?

Seunim: Yes, we <u>have</u>.

Anna:　Would it be possible to <u>come</u> this weekend?

Seunim: <u>I am sorry</u>. All reservations for this weekend are <u>full</u>.

Anna:　<u>How about next weekend?</u>

Seunim: Yes, would you like to <u>book</u> a reservation?

Anna:　<u>No thank you. I will do it myself on-line</u>.

Seunim: Ok, I <u>look forward to</u> seeing you next Saturday then.

⑤ 미국으로 전화하기

(스님이 미국으로 귀국한 잭에게 전화를 하려고 한다.)

스님1: 스님! 미국으로 전화하려면 어떻게 하면 되나요?

스님2: 먼저 국제전화번호를 누릅니다.

001, 002, 005, 00700 등 다양한 번호가 있습니다.

스님1: 그 다음엔요?

스님2: 다음엔 국가번호를 눌러야 합니다. 미국의 국가번호는 1번입니다.

스님1: 그럼 먼저 005를 누르고 다음에 1을 눌러야겠군요.

스님2: 다음엔 원하시는 번호를 누르시면 됩니다.

스님1: 그렇군요. 지역번호는 614, 전화번호는 201-4697.

아, 신호가 가네요.

Unit 5 | Calling to the USA

(A seunim tries to call Jack who has returned to the USA.)

Seunim1: Seunim, how can I call the USA?

Seunim2: First, you should dial the international telephone code.

There are many <u>international telephone codes</u> like zero zero one (001), zero zero two (002), zero zero five (005) or zero zero seven zero zero (00700).

Seunim1: Ok, after that?

Seunim2: Then you dial the country code. For the USA, it is one (1).

Seunim1: So I need to dial zero zero five (005) and one (1).

Seunim₂: Yes, followed by the number you wish to call.

Seunim₁: I see. The area code is six one four (614) and the number is two zero one dash four six nine seven (201-4697). Oh, it is ringing.

Words and Phrases

○ 어떻게 ~을 할 수 있나요? **How can I** + 동사?
이 시험에 어떻게 합격할 수 있나요? How can I pass this test?
어떻게 도와드릴까요? How can I help you?
조계사에 어떻게 갈 수 있나요? How can I get to Jogye-sa?

○ 국가번호 **country code**

○ 지역번호 **area code**

○ 전화번호 **telephone number**

○ 전화번호가 어떻게 되시나요? **What is your telephone number?**

○ 전화번호를 교환할까요? **Shall we exchange our telephone numbers?**

○ 앞으로 계속 안부를 주고받았으면 좋겠습니다 **I would like to keep in touch with you.**

○ 페이스북 관련 질문
페이스북을 사용하시나요? Are you on Facebook?
친구 신청을 보내주세요. Please send me a friend request.

○ 잘 도착했다고 꼭 연락주세요 **Let us know when you arrive safely.**

○ 잘 지내세요! **Take care! Take care of yourself!**

○ 잘 지내길 바랍니다 **I wish you well.**

Seunim₁: Seunim, how <u>would</u> I call the USA?

Seunim₂: First, you <u>can</u> dial the international telephone code.

There are many <u>options</u> like zero zero one (001), zero zero two (002), zero zero five (005) or zero zero seven zero zero (00700).

Seunim₁: <u>I see</u>, and after that?

Seunim₂: Then, <u>dial the</u> country code. For the USA, it is one (1).

Seunim₁: So I <u>should</u> dial zero zero two (002) and one (1).

Seunim₂: Yes, <u>and you can finally dial the</u> number you wish to call.

Seunim₁: <u>I got it</u>. The area code is six one four (614) and the number is two zero one dash four six nine seven (201-4697).

꽃은 섬돌 앞 내리는 비에 웃고

꽃은 섬돌 앞 내리는 비에 웃고
솔은 난간 밖의 바람에 운다
오묘한 지취를 찾으려 할 게 뭐 있나?
이것이 바로 원통법문이라네.

_벽송 지엄

Flowers Smile at the Rain on the Door Step

Flowers smile at the rain on the door step
Pines sing to the wind passing the balustrade
Why bother to seek marvelous teachings?
This is the teaching that penetrates true nature

_By Ven. Byeoksong Jieom

6 행사에 초대하기

애나: ABC무역회사입니다. 저는 애나입니다.

스님: 애나! 조계사의 무연 스님입니다.

애나: 아, 스님 안녕하세요?

스님: 네, 애나도 잘 지내셨지요?

애나: 네, 덕분에요.

스님: 이번에 우리 절에서 개산 100주년 기념으로 특별법회를 엽니다.
특별법문에 이어 전시회, 예술공연도 하니까 참석하면 유익한 시간이 될 겁니다.

애나: 그럼 꼭 가야지요. 언제 합니까?

스님: 자세한 것은 이메일로 보내겠습니다. 이메일 주소 좀 가르쳐주세요.

애나: 알겠습니다. 제 이메일은 lotus@buddhism.com입니다.

스님: 고맙습니다. 행복한 하루 보내시기 바랍니다.

애나: 네 스님, 감사합니다. 스님도요.

Unit 6 · Invitation to an Event

Anna: Thank you for calling ABC Trading, this is Anna.

Seunim: Anna! This is Muyeon Seunim from Jogye-sa.

Anna: Yes, Seunim. How are you?

Seunim: I am fine. I hope you are doing well.

Anna: Yes, thanks to you.

Seunim: Our temple is celebrating its 100th year anniversary with a special Dharma talk. Also, we will have an exhibition and artistic performances. If you can come, it would be great.

Anna: I'd love to come. When is the event?

Seunim: I can send you all the details by email. Can you tell me your email address?

Anna: Sure, it is lotus@buddhism.com.

Seunim: Thank you. I hope you have a pleasant day.

Anna: Yes Seunim. Thank you. Have a great day!

Words and Phrases

○ 덕분에 **Thanks to you**
덕분에 사업이 잘 되고 있습니다. Thanks to you, the business is going well.
덕분에 공부가 쉬워졌습니다. Thanks to you, studying is much easier.
덕분에 일이 잘 풀리고 있습니다. Thanks to you, things are going smoothly.

○ ~을 가르쳐 주세요 **Can you tell me** + 명사?
이름을 가르쳐 주세요. Can you tell me the name?
주소를 가르쳐 주세요. Can you tell me the address?
가는 길을 가르쳐 주세요. Can you tell me the direction?

○ ~으로 보내다 **send by** + 명사
이메일로 보내다. send by email.
팩스로 보내다. send by fax.
우편으로 보내다. send by regular mail.

○ 전시회 **Exhibition**

○ 초대장 **Letter of invitation**

○ 기념일 **Anniversary**

○ 정중히 모십니다 **You are cordially invited.**

○ 다시 한 번 더 말씀 드릴게요(전화번호, 주소, 또는 이메일 같은 정보 공유 시 자주 쓰임)
Let me repeat that for you.

Anna: ABC Trading, this is Anna. How may I help you?

Seunim: Anna! This is Seonjae Seunim from Jogye-sa.

Anna: Hello, Seunim. How have you been?

Seunim: I am doing well. How about you?

Anna: I am fine, thanks to you.

Seunim: Our temple is having a gathering for its 100-year anniversary with a special Dharma talk. Also, we will feature an exhibition and artistic performances. If you can join us, it would be great.

Anna: I'd love to join. What is the date?

Seunim: I would be happy to send you the information via email. What is your email address?

Anna: Wonderful! It is lotus@buddhism.com.

Seunim: Thank you. I hope you enjoy the day.

Anna: Thank you, Seunim. You as well.

64

한 잔의 차에 한 조각 마음이 나오니

한 잔의 차에 한 조각 마음이 나오니
한 조각 마음이 차 한 잔에 담겼네
자, 이 차 한 잔 마셔 보시게
한 번 맛보면 근심 걱정 모두 사라진다네.

_함허 득통

A Piece of Mind Arises from a Cup of Tea

A piece of mind arises from a cup of tea
A piece of mind is in the cup of tea
Please drink this cup of tea
One sip will bring about immeasurable joy

_By Ven. Hamheo Deuktong

1 사경

애나: 스님! 지금 하시는 게 무엇인가요?

스님: 사경을 하고 있습니다.

애나: 사경이 무엇인데요?

스님: 경전 구절을 한 글자씩 옮겨 쓰는 것으로써
  불교 수행 중의 하나지요.

애나: 이것은 한자네요?

스님: 예. 한글로 옮겨 쓰기도 합니다.

애나: 사경을 할 때는 어떤 마음가짐으로 하나요?

스님: 한 자 한 자 적을 때마다 마음을 집중하면서
  경전의 뜻을 가슴에 새긴답니다.

Unit 1 Copying Sutras

Anna: Seunim, what are you doing now?

Seunim: I am copying a sutra.

Anna: What do you mean?

Seunim: It is one of the Buddhist practices, to hand-copy a sutra word by word.

Anna: Are these Chinese characters?

Seunim: Yes, but you can also do it in Korean.

Anna: What kind of mind do you have to maintain when you do this?

Seunim: You concentrate on copying each word and try to bear the meaning
  of the sutra in your mind.

○ 무엇을 ~하세요(하고 계세요)?　**What are you –ing?**

무엇을 쓰세요?　What are you writing?

무엇을 생각하세요?　What are you thinking?

○ 필사하다　**Copy**

경전을 필사하고 있습니다.　I am copying a sutra.

이 육조단경은 돈황 필사본입니다.

This version of the *Platform Sutra* is from the Dunhuang manuscripts.

○ 한 글자씩, 한 단어씩　**word by word**

한 자 한 자, 또박또박 쓰세요.　Write neatly word by word.

한 글자씩 천천히 읽으세요.　Read slowly word by word.

○ 한자　**Chinese character**　/　중국어　**Chinese**

나는 한자 공부가 재미있다.　I like studying Chinese characters.

그는 중국어를 잘 구사한다.　He is good at speaking Chinese.

내 영국인 친구는 중국어를 참 잘한다.　My British friend is very good at Chinese.

○ 집중하다　**concentrate on (=focus on, pay attention to)**

호흡에 집중하세요.　Focus on your breathing.

강의에 집중하세요.　Please pay attention to the lecture.

○ 가슴에 새기다 / 명심하다　**keep/bear ~ in (one's) mind**

그 교훈을 가슴에 새기겠습니다.　I will keep the lesson in my mind.

공공장소에서는 조용히 대화하세요.　Keep in mind to speak quietly in public places.

○ 경전　**sutra**

반야심경　Heart Sutra　/　천수경　Thousand Hands Sutra　/　개경게　Sutra-Opening Chant

○ 수행　**practice**

참선수행　meditation practice　/　걷기명상　walking meditation

좌선　sitting meditation　/　묵언　noble silence

Pair Work　Practice by substituting the underlined words with other proper words and phrases.

Seunim: What did you just do, Anna?

Anna:　I hand-copied a sutra <u>in Chinese</u>.

Seunim: Oh, which sutra did you copy?

Dalli:　I did <u>the *Heart Sutra.*</u>

Seunim: That's nice. Do you do it regularly?

Dalli:　Yes, I do it <u>every morning</u>. But I still find it hard to <u>concentrate</u>.

Seunim: Everybody feels that way. You are doing just great.

② 법회 날

잭: 스님, 오늘은 절에 사람들이 많이 왔네요.

스님: 오늘은 음력 초하루라서 절에서 정기법회가 열리는 날입니다.
그리고 음력 보름(15일)에도 정기법회가 열린답니다.

잭: 기독교에서는 일요일마다 교회에 가는데
불교에서는 음력 초하루와 보름에 절에 가는군요.

스님: 요즘은 현대인의 생활양식에 맞추어서 일요일에 가족법회를 하는 절도 꽤 있습니다.

잭: 법회 날에는 무엇을 하나요?

스님: 경전도 읽고 찬불가도 부르고 스님의 법문도 듣지요.
법회가 끝나면 도반들과 함께 공양을 하면서 즐거운 시간을 가집니다.

Unit 2 On the Day of the Dharma Gathering

Jack: Seunim, there are many people at the temple today!

Seunim: Yes, it's because today is the first day of the month by the lunar calendar. It is when we have a regular Dharma gathering at the temple. We also have one on the fifteenth day.

Jack: I see. While Christians go to church every Sunday, Buddhists go to a temple on the first and fifteenth days of each month of the lunar calendar!

Seunim: But these days, to meet today's modern lifestyle, some temples offer Sunday Dharma gatherings for families.

Jack: What do you do on this day?

Seunim: You read sutras, sing Buddhist hymns, and listen to Dharma talks. After the gathering ends, you have lunch with your Dharma friends and enjoy yourself with them.

○ 음력/양력 **lunar/solar calendar**

내 생일은 음력으로 올해 2월이다. My birthday falls in February this year by the lunar calendar.

거의 모든 절에서는 음력을 사용한다. Most temples use the lunar calendar.

음력 초하루 the first day of the month by the lunar calendar, the first day of the lunar month

○ 법회 **Dharma assembly / Dharma gathering**

일요가족법회 Sunday Dharma gathering for families

어린이영어법회 Kids' English Dharma Class / 청년법회 Dharma gathering of young people

스님 법문 Dharma talk / 정기법회 regular Dharma gathering

○ ~에 부응하다. 맞추다 **meet, satisfy**

아이들은 엄마의 기대에 부응하기 위해 노력한다. Kids try hard to meet their moms' expectations.

누군가의 기대에 부응하기 위하여 살지 마세요.

Do not live your life to meet someone's expectations.

○ 현대 생활양식 **modern lifestyle**

현대 생활양식은 과거에 비해 편리하지만 많은 환경문제를 일으킨다.

The modern lifestyle is convenient compared to the past, but causes many environmental problems.

○ 주다, 제공하다 **offer**

부처님께 꽃 공양을 올리고 싶습니다. I would like to offer flowers to the Buddha.

몇몇 사찰에서 초심자들을 위하여 불교 교실을 운영합니다.

Some temples offer Buddhist classes for lay beginners.

○ ~와 즐거운 시간을 보내다 **enjoy oneself with~ (= have fun with)**

나는 오랜만에 휴가를 내서 제주도에서 즐거운 시간을 보냈다.

I got some days off after a long time and enjoyed myself on Jeju Island.

그 꼬마는 오늘 대각사에 있는 강아지와 즐겁게 놀았다.

That little kid had fun with the dog at Daegak-sa Temple today.

Pair Work Practice by substituting the underlined words with other proper words and phrases.

Michelle: Jack, do you go to the temple regularly?

Jack: Yes, I attend the Dharma gathering <u>on the first day of the month by the lunar calendar</u>.

What about you?

Michelle: Me, too, <u>but not on the first day of each month because of my work</u>.

Instead, I attend the <u>Sunday</u> Dharma gathering at <u>Bongeun-sa Temple</u>.

Jack: Did you make some good friends there?

I'm pleased that I decided to come.

Michelle: Yes, I did. I enjoy myself with them every <u>Sunday</u>.

③ 절 수행

애나: 스님! 저 여자분은 법당에서 왜 계속 절을 하고 있나요?

스님: 절 수행을 하고 있는 겁니다.

애나: 절을 하는 게 수행이라고요?

스님: 네, 절 수행은 자신의 마음을 낮추고 자신의 행동과 말과 마음씀을 참회하는 수행입니다.
또 '지금 여기'에 마음을 집중하는 데 매우 도움이 됩니다.

애나: 불상 앞에서 절을 하는 것은 우상숭배가 아닌가요?

스님: 그렇지 않아요. 불상 앞에서 절을 하는 이유는 우리에게 해탈을 길을 보여주고 깨달음의
길로 이끌어주시는 부처님의 은혜에 존경과 감사의 인사를 올리는 것입니다.
또한 모든 중생에게 불성이 있으므로 내 안에 계신 부처님께 절을 하는 것도 됩니다.

애나: 저도 한 번 해볼게요.
(잠시 후) 와! 운동도 많이 되겠어요. 막 땀이 나네요.

Unit 3 **Prostration Practice**

Anna: Seunim, why does that woman keep prostrating herself in the Buddha Hall?

Seunim: She is doing a prostration practice.

Anna: Are prostrations one of the Buddhist practices?

Seunim: Yes, it is. It helps you to keep a humble mind. While doing prostration practice, you can also look back and repent your actions, words and intentions. It also helps you to concentrate on the "here and now."

Anna: Isn't prostrating in front of the statue of the Buddha idolatry?

Seunim: No, it isn't. Prostrating in front of the statue of the Buddha means to pay respect and express gratitude to the Buddha who teaches us the path to liberation and leads us to the path to enlightenment.
In addition, since all sentient beings have buddha nature, it also equates to prostrating to the buddha within yourself.

Anna: Let me try!
(a little later) Wow, it is like exercising! I am already sweating.

○ 절 수행　**prostration practice**
매일 108배를 합니다.　I practice 108 prostrations every day.
집에서 매일 300배를 합니다.　I prostrate myself 300 times at home every day.

○ ~하도록 하는 데 도움이 된다　**be helpful for… to = help…to**
콧물을 멈추게 하는 데 도움이 된다.　It helps to stop your runny nose.
신심을 깊게 하는 데 도움이 된다.　It is helpful for you to deepen your faith.

○ ~를 하는 동안　**while**
밥을 먹으면서 책 보지 마세요.　Don't read books while eating.
우리가 스키를 타는 동안 그는 썰매를 탔다.　He rode a sled while we skied.

○ ~를 유지하다. 계속 ~한 상태로 있다　**stay + 형용사**
건강하세요.　Stay healthy.　　집중하세요.　Stay focused.

○ 우상숭배　**idolatry (=idol worship)**
어떤 이들은 불교가 우상숭배적이고 미신적이라고 비판합니다.
Some criticize that Buddhism is idolatrous and superstitious.

○ 대자대비하신 부처님　**the Buddha of Great Compassion**
불성　the buddha nature　／　중생　sentient beings

○ 마찬가지이다　**equates to, is equal to**
좋은 팀워크는 성공이나 마찬가지이다.　Good team work equates to success.
웃음은 건강과 행복이다.　Laughter is equal to good health and happiness.

○ ~ 해볼게요. ~하게 해주세요　**Let me try**
저 한번 해볼게요.　Let me try.
다시 한번 시도해볼게요.　Let me try it one more time.
이 신발 한번 신어볼게요.　Let me try these shoes on.

○ 참회하다　**repent**　／　참회　**repentance**
내 생각에 집착함으로써 상처를 입힌 모든 이들에게 참회하며 절합니다.
I prostrate myself in repentance to all those whom I have harmed through attachment to my thinking.
아픈 사람들에게 자비심을 내지 못한 저를 참회하며 절합니다.
I prostrate myself in repentance for my lack of compassion for the sick.

○ 신심, 신앙심　**faith**　／　신심있는　**faithful**
법문을 들으면 신심이 납니다.　I feel greater faith in Buddhism when I hear a Dharma talk.
내 도반은 참 신심이 깊습니다.　My Dharma friend is very faithful.

○ 땀나다　**sweat**
절을 하면 땀이 납니다.　Prostrations make you sweat.
땀이 나는 건 건강한 것입니다.　Sweating is good for your health.

Practice by substituting the underlined words with other proper words and phrases.

Michelle: Do you do prostration practice?

Dalli: Yes, I do <u>108</u> prostrations <u>every morning before I go to work</u>.

Michelle: Wow! That sounds great. Which temple do you go to?

Dalli: I go to <u>Silsang-sa Temple</u>.

Michelle: I would like to go with you some time. May I?

Dalli: Sure, why not?

아미타부처님은 어디에 계신가

아미타부처님 어디에 계신가?
가슴에 얹어 두고 잊지 말아라
생각이 다해 더는 생각할 수 없는 곳에 이르면
눈, 귀, 코, 입 온몸에서 붉은 금색광명 쏟아지리라.

Where Can I Find Amitabha Buddha?

Where can I find Amitabha Buddha?
Keep this question always in mind and never forget
When all thought is exhausted and you reach the state of non-thought
Red golden light will gush from your six sensory gates

4 청소(운력)

스님: 오늘은 절에 계신 모든 분들이 함께 청소를 하겠습니다.

잭: 스님, 저는 무엇을 하나요?

스님: 각자가 맡을 일을 여기 목록으로 만들었으니 참고하세요.

잭: 와, 저는 욕실 청소네요.

애나: 저는 마당 청소예요.

스님: 불교에서는 이렇게 함께 하는 일도 다 수행의 일부입니다.

애나: 그럼 청소만 함께 하나요?

스님: 아니요. 경우에 따라 이불 빨래나 방석 빨래도 함께 하고
농사짓는 절에서는 채마밭 가꾸기도 함께 합니다.
이렇게 함께 모여 청소나 일을 하는 걸 절에서는 '운력'이라고 한답니다.

Unit 4 **Cleaning (Communal Work)**

Seunim: Now, we are going to clean the temple altogether.

Jack: Seunim, what is my job?

Seunim: Please take a look at the list of who does what.

Jack: Wow! My job is to clean the bathroom.

Anna: Mine is to sweep the temple grounds.

Seunim: Working together like this is a part of Buddhist practice.

Anna: Then do we work together only when cleaning the temple?

Seunim: No, we also work together when washing the blankets and sitting cushions, and taking care of the vegetable garden during the farming season. To work or clean together in temples is referred to as "ullyeok" or "communal work."

○ ~을 보다 **take a look at (= look at), I wanted to experience ~.**
재미있는 체험을 하고 싶어서요. I wanted to experience something fun.
이 책 좀 한번 봐도 될까요? Can I take a look at this book?
이 꽃을 자세히 보세요. Please take a close look at this flower.

○ 누가 무엇을 하는지 **who does what**
이 프로젝트에 대한 업무분장을 정합시다. Let's decide who does what in this project.
누가 무엇을 하는지 표를 확인해보세요. Please check the list of who does what.

○ 포함하다 **include**
단체여행 비용에는 항공비, 숙박비, 아침식사비, 입장료가 포함됩니다.
The group tour fee includes airfare, accommodations, breakfasts and admission fees.

○ 가꾸다, 기르다, 돌보다 **take care of + 명사**
그는 아이들 돌보는 것을 좋아한다. He likes to take care of kids.
동생 잘 보고 있어라. Take good care of your little brother.

○ ~의 경우에 **in (the) case of / in case 주어 + 동사**
위급한 경우에 in case of emergency
상황이 변동될 경우를 대비해 두 번째 계획이 있어야 합니다.
There should be a plan B in case the situation changes.

○ 사찰 마당 **temple grounds**
사찰 마당을 청소하세요. Please clean the temple grounds.
빗자루로 마당을 쓰세요. Please sweep the grounds with a broom.

○ ~ 부분이다, ~ 일부다 **part of**
웃음은 내 삶의 일부이다. Laughter is part of my life.
직업은 내 수행의 일부이다. My profession is part of my practice.

○ 운력 **communal work**
절에서의 운력은 매일 아침에 진행됩니다. Communal work at temples is practiced every morning.
나는 절에서의 운력이 즐겁다. I like doing communal work at a temple.

Pair Work Practice by substituting the underlined words with other proper words and phrases.

Dalli: Have you done communal work before?
Michelle: Yes, I have done it <u>once</u> at <u>Silleuk-sa Temple</u>.
Dalli: What was your job?
Michelle: I <u>swept the temple grounds</u>.
Dalli: This time, our job is <u>to clean the toilet</u>.
Michelle: I see. Let's go for it!

⑤ 등 공양

잭: 스님, 법당에 왜 연등을 저렇게 많이 달아두는지요?

스님: 아, 불자들이 부처님오신날에 연등 공양을 올린 것입니다.

잭: 연등은 그날 하루만 올리는 것이 아닌가요?

스님: 대체로 1년등을 많이 하기 때문에 이렇게 걸어 둡니다.

잭: 등을 공양하는 이유는 무엇인지요?

스님: 등은 무지의 어둠을 밝히는 반야지혜를 상징하지요.

잭: 등불이 암흑을 밝히는 것처럼요?

스님: 그렇지요. 등불을 밝혀 다함께 지혜를 증득하자는 의미입니다.

잭: 그럼, 이 연등을 밝히는 유래는 어디에 있나요?

스님: 부처님 당시 아사세(아자따삿뚜) 왕이 부처님의 밤길을 밝혀드리기 위해
등불을 켠 데서 유래한답니다.

잭: 그야말로 어둠 속의 길을 밝히는 등불이군요.

스님: 그렇지요. 어둠 속에서도 등불이 길을 밝혀주니 목적지를 제대로 찾아갈 수 있는 거지요.

Unit 5 ## Offering Lanterns to the Buddha

Jack: Seunim, why are there so many lotus lanterns in the Buddha Hall?

Seunim: They are lanterns offered by Buddhists on the Buddha's Birthday.

Jack: Aren't they hung only on the very day of the Buddha's Birthday?

Seunim: Most lanterns remain hanging for one year.

Jack: Why do people offer lanterns?

Seunim: Lanterns symbolize great wisdom that lightens the darkness of ignorance.

Jack: Just like lanterns lighten the darkness?

Seunim: That's right. Lighting the lanterns signifies our wish to attain great wisdom.

Jack: Then, how did this tradition start?

Seunim: It started from when King Ajatasattu lit a lantern to help the Buddha on his nighttime journey.

Jack: Indeed, the lanterns lightening the darkness!

Seunim: That's right. As the lanterns lighten the path in the darkness, you can reach your correct destination.

Words and Phrases

○ 연등 **lotus lantern**
연등축제 Lotus Lantern Festival / 제등행렬 a lantern parade / 연등 공양 lotus lantern offering

○ 바로 그~ (강조하는 명사 앞에) **the very + 명사**
그녀가 바로 그 여자야. She is the very woman.
오늘이 바로 그 날이네! Today is the very day!

○ 상징하다 **symbolize**
불교에서 빛은 지혜를, 어둠은 무지를 상징한다.
In Buddhism, light symbolizes wisdom, and darkness symbolizes ignorance.

○ 의미하다 **signify (=mean)**
적색신호는 '멈춤'을 의미한다. A red light signifies 'stop'.

○ 밝게 하다, 비추다 **brighten, lighten**
등을 켜다. light a lantern (light의 과거형, 과거분사형: lit)
제등행렬을 위해 연등을 켰다. I lit a lantern for the lantern parade.
초를 켜서 방을 환하게 하자. Let's brighten the room by lighting some candles.

○ ~이 어떻게 시작되었습니까? **How did ~ start?**
이 풍습은 어떻게 시작되었나요? How did this custom start?
이 축제는 어떻게 시작되었나요? How did this festival start?

○ 밤길 통행 **nighttime journey, nocturnal journey**
가로등은 사람들의 밤길을 안전하게 하기 위해 설치된 것이다.
Streetlamps are set up for the safety of people traveling at night.

○ 목적지 **destination**
목적지까지 30분 남았습니다.
It will take about 30 minutes to our destination. / Our destination is 30 minutes away
목적지까지 7시간이 소요되었습니다. It took 7 hours until we reached our destination.

Free Response

1. What do most Buddhists do on the Buddha's Birthday?
2. What wish do lotus lanterns symbolize on the Buddha's Birthday?
3. How did the tradition of lighting lanterns start?
4. How can I offer lanterns to the Buddha?
5. Where is the Lotus Lantern Festival held and how can I get there?

6 기도

애나: 스님, 제가 요즘 회사에서 인간관계에 어려움이 있습니다.

스님: 그래요? 힘드시겠어요.

애나: 예, 스님. 그 사람이 없으면 참 좋겠다는 생각을 하곤 해요.

스님: 그러시겠지요.

애나: 그런데 현실적으로 그건 불가능하다는 것도 알아요.

스님: 현명한 생각이십니다.

애나: 불교에서는 모든 것이 '나'로부터 비롯한다고 하지요?

스님: 예, 먼저 애나가 그 사람을 대할 때 따뜻한 마음과 부드러운 말로 다가가면 어떨까요?

애나: 스님, 보기도 싫은데 어떻게 따뜻하게 대해요?

스님: 그럼 기도를 해보세요. 그 사람이 행복하라고 기도하면서, 내 마음에 자비심이 충만하게 해주십사고 해보세요.

Unit 6 **Prayer**

Anna: Seunim, I am having difficulties with someone at work these days.

Seunim: Is that so? That must be trying.

Anna: Yes, it is. I wish he would leave.

Seunim: I understand what you mean.

Anna: But, realistically, I know that is impossible.

Seunim: Very wise.

Anna: In the Buddhist teachings, everything comes from "I"?

Seunim: Correct. Anna, what about trying to approach him warm-heartedly with kind words first?

Anna: Seunim, how can I treat him warmly when I do not even want to look at him?

Seunim: Then, pray. Pray for his happiness and for compassion to fill your heart.

○ 어려움, 고난   **difficulties (= troubles)**
일이 잘 안 되어 힘듭니다.   I am having difficulties with my work
이 책 좀 한번 봐도 될까요?   Can I take a look at this book?
이 꽃을 자세히 보세요.   Please take a close look at this flower.

○ ~임에 틀림없다   **must**
사실임에 틀림없어.   This must be true!
그 가족은 분명 행복할거야.   That family must be happy.

○ 힘든, 괴로운   **trying, difficult, bad**
제가 힘든 상황에 처해 있어요.   I am in trying circumstances.
당신 때문에 매우 짜증이 나요.   You're a very trying person (difficult person).
그것은 건강에 나쁩니다.   It's bad for one's health.

○ ~하면 좋겠다(불가능한 소망)   **wish ~ would/could**
날 수 있으면 얼마나 좋을까!   I wish I could fly!
몇 년 더 젊어지면 얼마나 좋을까!   I wish I could become younger!

○ 실제로, 현실에는   **in reality**
실제로는 그렇게 작지 않다.   He is not that short in reality.
현실에는 그런 기술이 아직 없다.   There is no such technology in reality.

○ 따뜻한 마음으로   **warm-heartedly**
따뜻한 마음이 담긴 제스처   warm-hearted gestures
강아지를 냉정하게 대하지 마세요.   Please do not treat puppies cold-heartedly.

○ 어떻게 ~ 해요?   **How can I ~?**
어떻게 제가 그런 말을 해요?   How can I say such words?
제가 스님이 되려면 어떻게 하면 되나요?   How can I become a monk?

○ ~하는 반면, ~에 반하여   **while**
미나 언니는 키가 큰 반면 미나는 작다.   Mina is short while her older sister is tall.

○ 기도하다   **pray**
일체중생의 건강과 행복을 위해 기도합니다.   I pray for all sentient beings' health and happiness.
그는 그의 딸이 빨리 병에서 낫길 기도했다.
He prayed for his daughter to recover from the illness as soon as possible.

○ 자비(慈悲)는 본래 두 개 단어의 합성어이고 그 구성은 아래와 같다.
자(慈): maitrī : loving-kindness
비(悲): karuṇā : compassion
하지만 '자비'를 한 단어로 간주하는 경우도 종종 있는데 그럴 경우 'compassion'으로 표현한다.

Practice by substituting the underlined words with other proper words and phrases.

Michelle: What did you pray to the Buddha?

Dalli: I prayed <u>for my family's health and happiness.</u>
What about you?

Michelle: I prayed <u>for the well-being of African children who starve and suffer from wars.</u>

Dalli: That is such a beautiful prayer. I am very proud of you.

마음이
만 가지 경계를 따라서 굴러가니

마음이 만 가지 경계를 따라서 굴러가니
구르는 곳마다 참으로 심오하구나
흐름을 따라서 성품을 깨달으면
기쁨도 없고 근심도 없으리라.

_마나라

The mind follows
the revolutions of the percepts

The mind follows the revolutions of the percepts,
But where they revolve in reality is obscured.
By following the flow (of the percepts)
one can recognize and attain their nature,
Which has neither joy nor grief.

_By Ven. Manorhita

Chapter 5

Buddhist Pilgrimages 성지 순례

① 성지 순례 안내

스님: 이번 토요일에는 남해 보리암으로 성지 순례를 갑니다.

잭: 남해안 바닷가에 있는 절이지요?

스님: 그래요. 3대 관음성지 중 하나지요.

잭: 3대 관음성지는 무엇인가요?

스님: 모두 바닷가에 있는 절로 사람들이 관세음보살님께 기도를 올리러 많이 찾는 곳입니다.
3대 관음성지로는 이 밖에도 낙산사 홍련암, 강화 보문사가 있지요.

잭: 와, 전부 가보면 좋겠네요.

스님: 성지 순례는 단순한 여행이 아닙니다.

잭: 저는 떠날 생각을 하니까 벌써 홀가분한데요?

스님: 성지순례는 부처님과 옛 성현들의 발자취를 찾아가는 것입니다.
번뇌에 찌든 마음을 내려놓고 수행정진을 하는 또 다른 방법 중 하나이지요.

Buddhist Pilgrimage Announcement

Seunim: This Saturday's pilgrimage destination is Bori-am in Namhae.

Jack: The temple on the coast of the South Sea?

Seunim: Yes. It is one of the Three Great Avalokitesvara Temples.

Jack: What do you mean by the Three Great Avalokitesvara Temples?

Seunim: They are temples located by the sea where the Avalokitesvara Hall is frequented by people offering prayers. The other two temples are Hongnyeon-am of Naksan-sa Temple and Bomun-sa on Ganghwa Island.

Jack: Wow, I'd like to visit all of them.

Seunim: A pilgrimage to a temple is not like an ordinary trip.

Jack: Thinking of visiting there already makes me feel free and easy!

Seunim: In Buddhist pilgrimages we retrace the footsteps of the Buddha and old sages. We set aside our afflictions and refocus our mind on our practice.

- 불교성지 순례　**Buddhist pilgrimage**

- 3대 관음성지　**The Three Great Avalokitesvara Temples**

- 관세음보살　**Avalokitesvara (Bodhisattva of Compassion)**
- 지장보살　**Ksitigarbha (Earth Storehouse Bodhisattva, Bodhisattva of Hell)**
- 대세지보살　**Mahasthamprapta (Bodhisattva of Great Power and Wisdom)**

- 홀가분하다　**feel free and easy (=feel light-hearted)**
  숙제를 다 끝내니 홀가분합니다.　I feel light-hearted after finishing the homework.
  산에 가면 홀가분해집니다.　I feel free and easy in the mountains.

- 발자취를 따라가다　**retrace the footsteps (=course, path) of ~**
  고승 원효의 발자취를 따라가는 불교성지 순례
  A Buddhist pilgrimage that retraces the path of the eminent monk, Wonhyo

- 내려놓다　**put down, set aside, cast aside (= 비우다. empty)**
  모든 고통스러운 감정을 내려놓으세요.　Put down all of your afflictive emotions.
  마음을 비워야 일이 잘 된다.　Things go better when you empty your mind.

- 일반적인, 일상적인　**ordinary, general, mundane**
  특별한, 특출한　extraordinary, special
  일상이 행복해야 진짜 행복한 것입니다.　You are truly happy only when you are happy in your daily life.
  그녀는 수학에 특출하다.　She is extraordinary in math.

- 번뇌　**afflictions**
  번뇌에 찌든 여러분의 마음을 들여다보세요.　Look into your afflicted minds.
  명상을 통해 마음을 번뇌의 속박에서 풀어주는 법을 익힐 수 있다.
  Through meditation we can become skilled at freeing our minds from the influence of afflictions.

Pair Work　Practice by substituting the underlined words with other proper words and phrases.

Michelle: Where shall we go <u>during this weekend?</u>

Yoon:　Let's go to <u>Naksan-sa Temple</u>. It's one of the Four Great Avalokitesvara Temples.

Michelle: That is a good idea. I've been to <u>Bori-am</u>, and it was very nice.

Yoon:　<u>Just talking about it</u> already makes me <u>feel excited</u>.

② 참가자의 문의사항

애나: 아침 몇 시까지 모이나요?

스님: 6시 반까지 조계사 앞에 오시면 관광버스가 기다리고 있을 겁니다.
참가하실 분은 신청서를 작성해 주세요.

애나: 여기 주민등록번호도 쓰라고 되어 있네요?

스님: 예, 여행자보험을 들어야 하니까요. 외국인은 여권번호를 쓰시면 됩니다.

애나: 스님! 당일로 돌아올 수 있나요?

스님: 예, 늦은 밤에 서울에 도착할 겁니다.

애나: 그 밖에 주의사항이 있나요?

스님: 편안한 옷차림에 등산화나 운동화를 착용하세요.
아침, 점심과 물은 다 제공되므로 따로 준비하지 않아도 됩니다.

Participants' Questions

Anna: What time do we meet in the morning?

Seunim: Please come by 6:30a.m. There will be a bus waiting in front of Jogye-sa Temple. Those who want to apply, please, fill out the application form.

Anna: There's a section for resident registration number.

Seunim: Yes, it is for insurance purposes. Non-Koreans may write their passport number.

Anna: Seunim, is it a day trip?

Seunim: Yes, we will be back in Seoul by that night.

Anna: Is there anything else I have to know?

Seunim: Please put on comfortable clothes and hiking boots or sneakers. Breakfast, lunch and water will be provided, so don't worry about those things.

○ ~ 서류(신청서)를 작성하다　**fill out a form (application form)**

템플스테이를 신청하고자 하시는 분은 이 신청서를 쓰십시오.
Those who want to apply for the Templestay program, please fill out this form.

신청서를 써서 저에게 제출해주세요.　Please fill out the form and submit it to me.

○ 주민등록번호　**resident registration number, Korean national ID number**

외국인등록번호　alien registration number

○ 보험에 가입하다　**buy (take out) insurance**

저는 생명보험을 가지고 있어요.　I have life insurance.

보험을 해지하고 싶습니다.　I would like to cancel my insurance.

보험으로 처리하겠습니다.　I'll deal with it through my insurance

○ 당일 여행　**a day trip, one-day trip**

이 여행은 1박 2일입니다.　It is a trip for one night and two days.

당일 여행은 일찍 출발합니다.　A day trip leaves early in the morning

○ 그 밖에 더…　**anything else, something else**

더 필요한 거 없으세요?　Do you need anything else?

드리고 싶은 것이 더 있습니다.　I have something else to give you.

○ ~까지 오세요　**Please come by….**

정오 전에 오세요.　Please come before noon.

5시 이후에 오세요.　Please come after 5p.m.

○ 등산화　**hiking boots**　/　운동화　**sneakers, tennis shoes, running shoes**

절에서 하이힐을 신으면 걷기가 힘듭니다.　It is difficult to walk if you wear high heels to temples.

샌들 sandals, 슬리퍼 slippers, 하이힐 high heels, 장화 boots, 우화 rain boots

---

Pair Work　Practice by substituting the underlined words with other proper words
and phrases.

Yoon:　What time do you usually wake up in the morning?

Mina:　I usually wake up at 7:30. But I have to wake up at 5:30
tomorrow morning.

Yoon:　Why so early?

Mina:　I applied for a Buddhist pilgrimage to Mita-sa Temple
in Jeollanamdo. I have to be in front of City Hall by 6:30.

Yoon:　I see. What time will you be back?

Mina:　I will be back by 9:00 p.m.

Yoon:　Have a nice time!

출발하는 날

잭: (조계사 앞에서 혼잣말을 하는 잭) 여기가 조계사 앞인데 버스는 어디 있을까?
　　아 저기다! 앞에 '남해 보리암'이라고 써 있네.

애나: (버스기사에게 묻는다) 이거 남해 보리암 가는 버스지요?

버스기사: 예, 어서 타세요.

잭: (애나 옆자리를 가리키며) 여기 사람 있어요?

애나: 아니요.

잭: 그럼 앉아도 되겠지요?

애나: 그럼요.

애나: 그런데 5분밖에 안 남았는데 빈 자리가 많네요.

잭: 사람들이 좀 늦나 봅니다.

스님: (6시 40분이 되어) 다들 오셨나요?

총무: 아직 두 분이 안 왔습니다.

Unit 3 ## On the Morning of Departure

Jack:　(talking to himself at Jogye-sa Temple) I am in front of Jogye-sa Temple. Where is the bus? Oh, there! I see the sign that reads "Bori-am in Namhae."

Anna:　(asking the bus driver) Is this bus going to Bori-am in Namhae?

Driver :　Yes, that's right. Please get on.

Jack:　(pointing to the seat next to Anna) Is this seat taken?

Anna:　No, it isn't.

Jack:　May I sit here?

Anna:　Of course. We have only 5 minutes left, but there still seems to be more vacant seats.

Jack:　Maybe people are late.

Seunim:　(at 6:40) Are we all present?

Manager: Two people have not yet come

○ 혼잣말하다　**talk to oneself**
나는 혼잣말하면서 생각을 정리한다.　While talking to myself, I collect my thoughts.
혼잣말은 좋은 습관이 아니다.　Talking to oneself is not a good habit.

○ 표지판　**sign, signboard**
표지판이 없네요.　I don't see any signs.
표지판에 '종로 3가'라고 써 있나요?　Does the signboard read "Jongno-3ga"?

○ 이 버스 ~로 가나요?　**Is this bus going to~?**
이 버스는 종로로 가나요?　Is this bus going to Jongno?
이 기차는 원주로 가나요?　Is this train going to Wonju?

○ ~ 인 것 같다　**seem to…**
이 사찰은 알려지지 않은 것 같다.　This temple seems to be unknown to people.
이 사찰에는 관광객이 참 많은 것 같다.　This temple seems to have many tourists.

○ 빈자리 / 주인 있는 자리　**vacant seat / taken seat**
이 자리 비어 있나요?　Is this seat vacant (not taken yet)?
이 자리 사람 있어요.　I am afraid it is taken.

○ 출석한, 참석한　**present (↔ 반의어 absent)**
미나는 출석했고, 민정이는 결석했다.　Mina was present, and Minjeong was absent.
나는 그 회의에 참석했다.　I was present at the meeting.

○ 아직　**yet**
존이 아직 집에 오지 않았습니다.　John has not come back home yet.
아직 꽃이 피지 않았습니다.　The flowers have not yet blossomed.

Pair Work　Practice by substituting the underlined words with other proper words and phrases.

(at a bus station)

Michelle:　(to a bus driver) Is this bus going to the <u>Namsan Library?</u>

Bus Driver:　No, it isn't. <u>Take bus 402.</u>

Michelle:　Thank you!

(on bus 402)

Michelle:　Is this seat taken?

Passenger:　<u>No, it isn't. Please…</u>

Michelle:　Thank you!

옆자리 도반과의 대화

애나: 성지 순례 많이 가봤어요?

잭: 아니요, 이번이 처음이라서 기대가 많이 됩니다.

애나: 저는 보리암에 전에 한 번 가본 적이 있어요.
'비단산'이라는 의미인 금산에 있는데 참 아름다웠어요.

잭: 날씨가 참으로 좋네요. 하늘도 맑고...

애나: 저기 보세요! 벚꽃도 활짝 피었어요.

잭: 한국에 오신 지는 얼마나 되었어요?

애나: 6개월 정도요. 잭은요?

잭: 저는 3개월 전에 왔어요.

Unit 4 **Conversation with a Dharma Friend Sitting Next to You**

Anna: Have you taken part in a pilgrimage before?

Jack: No, this is my first time. I am very much looking forward to it.

Anna: I've been to Bori-am before. It's located on Mt. Geumsan which means "Silk Mountain." It was indeed beautiful.

Jack: The weather is nice! The sky is blue...

Anna: Look! The cherry blossoms are in full bloom.

Jack: How long have you been in Korea?

Anna: About 6 months. What about you?

Jack: I came to Korea 3 months ago.

○ 전에 ~해본 적 있으세요?　**Have you ~ before?**
템플스테이에 참석해본 적 있으세요?　Have you tried a Templestay before?
영국에 가본 적 있으세요?　Have you visited Britain before?

○ 참가하다　**take part in (= participate in)**
나는 작년 여름수련법회에 참가했다.　I participated in last year's Summer Dharma Camp.
제등행렬에 참가하자.　Let's take part in the lantern parade!

○ 기대하다, ~을 즐거운 마음으로 기다리다　**look forward to 동사-ing / 명사**
그를 만나기를 고대하고 있다.　I am looking forward to meeting him.
부처님오신날이 기대됩니다.　I look forward to the Buddha's Birthday!

○ ~에 위치해 있다　**be located in ~**
송광사는 전라남도에 있다.　Songgwang-sa is located in Jeollanamdo.
남산은 서울의 한복판에 위치해 있다.　Mt. Namsan is located in the center of Seoul.

○ 정말, 참으로　**indeed** (강조)
그녀는 정말로 매력적이었다.　She was indeed charming.
그는 정말로 행복해 보였다.　He looked indeed happy.

○ 활짝 핀　**in full bloom**
다양한 종류의 꽃들이 만개하였다.　Various flowers are in full bloom.
라일락이 활짝 피었다.　The lilacs are in full bloom.

○ 넌 어때?　**How (What) about you?**
전 아이가 한 명인데 당신은요?　I have one kid, and what about you?
전 햄버거 먹을 건데 어떠세요?　I'd like to have a burger, and how about you?

Pair Work　Practice by substituting the underlined words with other proper words and phrases.

Yoon: Have you been to <u>Mt. Bukhan-san</u> before?

Michelle: No, I haven't.

Yoon: What do you think of hiking there <u>this Saturday?</u>

Michelle: Where is it located?

Yoon: It is located <u>north of Seoul</u>. We can get off <u>at Gireum Station on line 4</u>.

Michelle: Alright. Let's meet there at <u>9:00 a.m.</u>

Yoon: I am already looking forward to it!

⑤ 휴게소

총무: (안내 방송을 한다) 우리 버스는 곧 휴게소에 도착합니다.

　　　 휴식 시간으로 10분을 드릴 테니 8시 30분까지 버스로 돌아와주십시오.

잭: 화장실이 급했는데 잘 되었네요.

애나: 저도요. 우리 스낵코너 앞에서 만나기로 해요.

잭: (스낵코너 앞에서) 애나 뭐 드실래요?

애나: 저는 커피하고 감자 먹을래요.

잭: 호두과자도 먹죠. 다같이 나누어 먹게 좀 넉넉히 사야겠어요.

애나: 어머, 시간이 다 됐어요.. 어서 가요.

Unit 5　At a Highway Service Area

Manager: (announcement) We will soon be at the service area.

　　　　　 We will rest there for 10 minutes. Please come back by 8:30.

Jack: That's good news. I wanted to go to the toilet.

Anna: Same here. Let's meet in front of that snack bar.

Jack: (In front of the snack bar) Anna, what would you like to have?

Anna: I'd like a cup of coffee and some potatoes.

Jack: Let's get some walnut-shaped cakes, too.

　　　 It'll be better to buy some more to share them with others.

Anna: Time is almost up. Let's hurry.

○ 고속도로 휴게소 **highway service area**
   동의어 expressway rest area

○ 공지, 안내 **announcement (= notice)**
   공지사항이 있겠습니다. I have some announcements.

○ '동감이다' **Same here**의 다양한 표현
   Me too. / Ditto. / So do (am) I. / I agree with you. / You said it!!
   I know. / I think so, too. / That's what I mean. / That's my point.

○ 무엇으로 하시겠습니까? 뭐 드실래요? **What would you like to have?**
   무엇으로 주문하시겠습니까? What would you like to order?
   음료는 무엇으로 드릴까요? What would you like to drink?
   에그베이컨 샌드위치로 할게요. I'd like a sandwich with eggs and bacon.
   커피 주세요. I'd like a cup of coffee, please.

○ 호두과자 **walnut-shaped cake**
   천안은 호두과자로 유명한 도시다. Cheonan is a city famous for walnut-shaped cakes.

○ 시간이 (거의) 다 되었다. **Time is (almost) up.**
   시간이 없다. Time is running out. / We don't have much time. / We are pressed for time.
   시간이 많다. We have a lot of time.
   꾸물거릴 시간이 없다. We have no time to waste (lose).

○ 서두르다. **hurry**
   서두르자. Let's hurry.
   서둘러! Hurry up!
   서두르지 마세요. 천천히 하세요. Don't hurry. Take it easy.

Pair Work   Practice by substituting the underlined words with other proper words and phrases.

Dalli: It'll be good to visit grandmother soon. I am worried about her.

Cousin: <u>Same here</u>. She's been so weak. Let's go tomorrow.

Dalli: Alright. Shall we meet <u>in front of the bus terminal at 11:00 a.m.?</u>

Cousin: OK. Do you know what she likes to <u>eat?</u>

Dalli: I think she likes <u>walnut-shaped cakes.</u>

Cousin: I see. We can buy some on the way at a <u>service area.</u>

⑥ 성지 도착

스님: 장시간 버스 타느라고 힘드셨지요?
자 이제부터 보리암을 향하여 산을 올라가겠습니다.

총무: 앞에 한 사람, 뒤에 한 사람 인도자가 있으니 따라가시면 됩니다.
대열에서 너무 벗어나진 마시고요.

스님: 보리암에 도착하면 대웅전에 참배한 후 잠시 주지스님 말씀이 있을 거예요.
먼저 도착하신 분은 대웅전 앞에서 기다려주세요.

총무: 자 출발합니다!

잭: 이름이 '비단산(금산)'이라더니 정말 산이 아름답네요.

애나: 곳곳에서 남해바다를 한눈에 볼 수 있어서 더욱 좋아요.
얼른 올라가서 해수관음상에 참배를 합시다.

Unit 6 **Arrival at the Temple**

Seunim: You must feel tired from the long bus journey.
From here, we will hike up the mountain to Bori-am.

Manager: There will be one guide in front and another in back.
Please follow them and try not to get out of line too much.

Seunim: At Bori-am, we will pay homage in the Hall of Avalokitesvara
and listen to the abbot's Dharma talk. Please wait in front of
the hall in case you arrive first.

Manager: Alright. Let's set off.

Jack: I totally agree with the name Silk Mountain! It's beautiful.

Anna: It's even more wonderful as you have a view of the South Sea
from any place. Let's go and pay homage to the Avalokitesvara
Statue that looks out over the sea.

○ 등산하다 **hike**
나는 등산을 좋아합니다. I like hiking.
우리 식구들은 일요일마다 등산합니다. My family hikes every Sunday.

○ 앞에서 **in front** / 뒤에서 **at the back, in back, at the rear**
옆에서 by the side of, on the side, beside
경찰이 우리를 앞에서, 뒤에서, 옆에서 막았다. Policemen blocked us in front, in back, and on both sides.

○ 대열에서 이탈하다 **get out of the line**
대열에서 낙오한 사람이 한 명 있었다. There was one person who fell far behind the line.
저는 대열의 맨 끝에 있습니다. I am the last in line.
한 줄로 걸으세요. Walk in a line.

○ 참배하다 / 경의를 표하다 **pay homage to (= pay one's respects to / worship)**
당신의 노고에 경의를 표합니다. I pay my respects to your efforts.
관세음보살님께 참배합니다. I pay homage to the Bodhisattva Avalokitesvara.

○ 관음전 **Hall of Avalokitesvara**
○ 대웅전 **Main Buddha Hall**
○ 극락전 **Hall of Amitabha Buddha, Hall of Ultimate Bliss**
○ 지장전 **Hall of Ksitigarbha**

○ 출발하다. 떠나다 **set off (= set out, depart, leave, take off)**
새벽 5시에 출발하였다. We set off at 5:00 in the morning.
비행기가 밤 8시에 출발했다. The airplane took off at 8:00 in the evening.

○ 동의하다 **agree with**
당신의 의견에 동의합니다. I agree with your opinion.
그의 생각에 동의할 수 없다. I cannot agree with his thoughts.

Pair Work Practice by substituting the underlined words with other proper words and phrases.

Dalli: Have you been to Mt. Bugak-san?

Yoon: Yes, I've hiked there once. It was very rocky.

Dalli: The name of the mountain means "rocky mountain north of Seoul."

Yoon: Interesting! I totally agree with the name! But I enjoyed hiking there.

Chapter 6

Korean Buddhist History and Culture
한국불교의 역사와 문화

1 천 년 고찰

잭: 스님, 보리암을 왜 천 년 고찰이라고 하나요?

스님: 천 년이 넘는 역사를 가진 절이니까요.
보리암은 신라 신문왕 3년(683년)에 지은 절입니다.

잭: 천 년이라면 정말로 상상하기 어려운 오랜 세월이군요.
한국엔 천 년 고찰이 많은가요?

스님: 많지요. 불교를 국교로 했던 신라시대나 고려시대 초기에 지은 절이 많으니까요.

잭: 한국에서 가장 오래된 절은 어디에 있나요?

스님: 전남 나주시에서 27킬로미터 떨어진 곳에 있는 불회사랍니다.
백제 침류왕 1년(384년) 인도승 마라난타가 세웠다고 전해지고 있죠.

Unit 1 ## Millennial Temples

Jack: Seunim, why is Bori-am called a millennial temple?

Seunim: It's because it has more than 1,000 years of history.
Bori-am was built in 683, the 3rd year of the reign of King Sinmun in the Silla Dynasty.

Jack: 1,000 years is absolutely an unimaginable length of time! Are there many temples of that age in Korea?

Seunim: Yes, there are quite a few. That's because Buddhism was established as the state religion of the Silla and Goryeo Dynasties.

Jack: Where is the oldest temple located in Korea?

Seunim: It is 27km away from the city of Naju in Jeollanamdo, and it's called Bulhoe-sa. It is known that the temple was built by Marananta, an Indian Buddhist monk, in the first year of the reign of King Chimnyu in the Baekje Kingdom.

○ 천 년 고찰 **a millennial temple, a thousand-year-old temple**
백 년 된 집 a hundred-year-old house

○ ~라고 불리다 **be called ~**

○ 관세음보살 **Avalokitesvara (Bodhisattva of Compassion)**
젊은 가수 그룹들을 일반적으로 한국에서는 '아이돌'이라고 부른다.
Youth singing groups are generally called "idols" in Korea.

○ 통치 기간에 **in (during) the reign of**
세종이 통치하는 동안 조선에는 풍년이 많았다.
During the reign of King Sejong, Joseon enjoyed good harvests for many years.
불교는 한반도에 고구려 소수림왕 2년에 처음 들어왔다.
Buddhism was first introduced to the Korean peninsula in the 2nd year of the reign of King Sosurim in the Goguryeo Kingdom.

○ 상상할 수 없는 **unimaginable**
생각할 수 없는 unthinkable
표현할 수 없는 indescribable
말로 설명할 수 없는 unexplainable

○ 많은 **quite a few** (셀 수 있는 경우), **quite a bit of** (셀 수 없는 경우)
동의어 many, quite a number, not a few, quite a lot of
나에겐 좋은 친구들이 많이 있다. I have quite a few good friends.
꽤 많은 돈이 갑자기 나에게 들어왔다. Quite a bit of money came to me all of a sudden.

○ 국교 **state religion**
1948년 이후 한국은 국교가 없어졌다. Korea has had no state religion since 1948.
불교는 오랫동안 한반도의 국교였다.
Buddhism was the state religion on the Korean peninsula for a long time.

○ ~로 알려져 있다. **be known that~, be known as~**
독도는 한국의 섬으로 알려져 있다. Dokdo is known as a Korean island.
붉은 육류는 성인병을 유발하는 것으로 알려져 있다. Red meats are known to cause adult diseases.

Free Response

1. Why are there so many 1,000-year-old temples in Korea?
2. When was Bori-am built, and who was the king at that time?
3. Who built the oldest temple in Korea and where is it?
4. Why does Korea no longer have a state religion?
5. In Korean history, what were the benefits of Buddhism being the state religion?

② 사찰음식

애나: 스님! 요즘 세계적으로 채식이 붐을 이루고 있어요.

스님: 그래요?

애나: 그런데 스님들은 아주 오래전부터 채식을 하고 계시잖아요.

스님: 스님들이 채식을 많이 하지만 초기 계율에는 육식을 허용하고 있죠.
부처님과 부처님의 제자들은 일생 동안 신도님들에게 공양받은 것을 먹어야 했거든요.

애나: 아, 선택의 기회가 없었군요. 그런데 요즘 사찰음식은 모두 채식이지 않나요?

스님: 그렇습니다. 스님들이 절에서 음식을 만들어 먹기 시작하면서
완전히 채식을 하게 되었지요.

애나: 그렇군요. 채식의 장점도 많지요?

스님: 몸과 마음을 맑게 해주지요. 또 환경보존에도 도움이 되고요.

Unit 2 The Vegetarian Diet of Buddhist Monks

Anna: Seunim, vegetarian diets are very popular worldwide these days.

Seunim: Is that so?

Anna: But Buddhist monks have already practiced it for a long time.

Seunim: You're right, but the early precepts had allowed eating meat.
The reason was that the Buddha and his disciples had to eat
whatever devotees offered them.

Anna: I see. They didn't have much choice. However, isn't temple food
all vegetarian these days?

Seunim: Yes, it is. As monastics began to cook their own food at temples,
temple food became wholly vegetarian.

Anna: Really? There must be some advantages of a vegetarian diet.

Seunim: It keeps your body and mind clear and helps preserve the natural
environment.

○ 붐, 대유행(명사), 호황을 누리다(동사)　**boom, be very popular, be very trendy**

한국의 80년대에는 아파트 붐이 있었다.　There was an apartment-building boom in the 1980s in Korea.

짧은 바지가 요즘 대유행이다.　Short pants are very popular these days.

○ 계율　**precepts**

계율을 지키는 것은 모든 것의 기본입니다.　Keeping the precepts is basic for all Buddhists.

오계를 지키세요.　Keep the five precepts.

○ 식단　**diet**

저는 다이어트 중이에요.　I am on a diet.

저는 채식을 합니다.　I am on a vegetarian diet.

cf. 채식의 종류

• Vegan: 고기, 생선, 우유, 달걀 등 일체 동물에서 얻은 것은 먹지 않는 채식주의자

• Lacto vegetarian: (고기, 생선, 달걀은 먹지 않고) 유제품은 먹는 채식주의자

• Ovo vegetarian: (고기, 생선, 유제품은 먹지 않고) 달걀은 먹는 채식주의자

• Lacto-Ovo vegetarian: (고기, 생선은 먹지 않고) 달걀, 유제품은 먹는 채식주의자

○ 얼마나 ~한지 모르는구나　**You don't know how + 형용사**

네가 얼마나 행복한 아이인지 모르는구나.　You don't know how happy you are.

얼마나 비싼 것인지 모르는구나.　You don't know how valuable this is.

○ 장점, 강점, 이익　**advantage**

동의어　merit, strong point

반대어　disadvantage, weak point

○ 보존하다　**preserve**

숲을 보존하는 데 힘을 보태주세요.　Please support forest preservation

Free Response

1. What are the advantages of having a vegetarian diet?

2. What do you think are the reasons for the worldwide boom in vegetarianism?

3. How do you like vegetarian dishes?

4. What is your favorite vegetarian dish?

5. Why did the early precepts allow eating meat?

③ 세계로 전파되는 한국 사찰음식

잭: 스님! 한국 사찰음식에 대한 전시와 시식회가 파리 유네스코빌딩에서 열렸다고 합니다.

스님: 그것 좋은 소식이네요.
작년에는 미국 뉴욕에서도 한국 사찰음식 행사가 열렸지요.

잭: 와! 한국 사찰음식이 세계로 전파되는군요.

스님: 이렇게 건강하고 영양도 균형 잡힌 요리가 세계화되면
세계인의 식생활에도 기여하는 셈이지요.

잭: 스님, 저도 사찰음식 팬이에요. 절에서 먹는 음식도 좋고,
사찰음식 전문점에서 먹는 음식도 맛있어요.

스님: 그럼 잭이 돌아가서 한국 사찰음식 홍보대사를 하면 되겠네요.

Unit 3   Korean Buddhist Temple Food Spreading to the World

Jack: Seunim, there was recently a Korean Buddhist temple food exhibition and tasting event at the UNESCO building in Paris.

Seunim: That is such good news. Last year, it was held in New York in the U.S.

Jack: Wow! Korean Buddhist temple food is spreading all over the world!

Seunim: Spreading temple food worldwide will be Korea's contribution to the world's healthy dietary life.

Jack: Seunim, I am also a fan of temple food. I love the foods at temples and those served at temple food restaurants.

Seunim: You could be an ambassador for Korean Buddhist temple food once you go back!

○ 한국 사찰음식 **Korean Buddhist temple food**

○ **UNESCO**(United Nations Educational, Scientific and Cultural Organization)

○ 참~ (강조의 용법) **such + 형용사**
참 좋은 소식이네. It is such good news.
참 행복한 행사였다. It was such a happy event.

○ ~에서 개최되었다 **~ was held in ~**
2012년 엑스포는 여수에서 열렸다. The 2012 Expo was held in Yeosu.
2002년 월드컵은 한국과 일본에서 열렸다. The 2002 World Cup was held in Korea and Japan.

○ 전 세계로 **all over the world (= worldwide, throughout the world)**
전국으로 all over the country
전국 방방곡곡으로 every corner (part) of the country

○ 좋아하다. 팬이다 **be a fan of ~ (= love, like very much)**
내 미국인 친구는 K-Pop의 열성 팬이다. My American friend is a big fan of K-Pop.
나는 이탈리아 음식을 좋아한다. I am a fan of Italian foods.

○ ~할 수 있을 것이다(현실이 아닌 상황에서의 가능성을 나타낼 때) **could**
원하기만 하면 그는 해결할 수 있어. He could fix it if only he wanted to.
열심히 하면 잘할 수 있을 거야. You could do it well if you tried hard enough.

○ 홍보대사 **(honorary) ambassador**
장동건은 생명나눔실천본부의 홍보대사로 활동하고 있다.
Jang Dong-geon is an honorary ambassador for the organization called "Life Share Practice Association".

Pair Work   Practice by substituting the underlined words with other proper words and phrases.

Dalli: Michelle, did you see the movie "Spring, Summer, Fall, Winter and Spring"?

Michelle: Yes, I watched it. I thought it was such a beautiful movie.

Dalli: Do you think so?

Michelle: I am a big fan of the director, so I love all of his movies.

Dalli: I will go home and watch it tonight.

④ 다선일미

스님: 애나! 이리 오세요. 차를 우리고 있으니 함께 들어요.

애나: 와! 향이 좋아요.

스님: 그래요? 맛도 좋을 겁니다.

애나: 자그마한 다구들도 참 예쁩니다.

스님: 선승들은 차를 아주 좋아합니다.

애나: 차가 맛이 있어서 그런가요?

스님: 그렇기도 하지만 예부터 다선일미(茶禪一味)라는 말이 있어요.
차와 참선은 한 가지 맛이라는 뜻이지요.

애나: 그게 무슨 뜻인가요?

스님: 차와 선은 깊이 직접 체험한 사람만이 알 수 있고
말로 설명할 수 없는 영역에 있다는 것이 아닐까요.

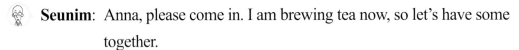

Unit 4 **Daseon-Ilmi (The One Exquisite Flavor of Tea and Seon)**

Seunim: Anna, please come in. I am brewing tea now, so let's have some together.

Anna: Wow! It smells nice.

Seunim: Does it? I bet it tastes nice too.

Anna: These small tea utensils are very cute and pretty.

Seunim: Seon monks enjoy tea a lot.

Anna: Is it because of its nice taste?

Seunim: Yes, it could be. But as an old dictum, "Daseon-Ilmi," goes, "for Buddhist monks, tea and meditation have the same flavor."

Anna: What does it mean?

Seunim: I think it means that both tea and meditation fall under the realm of inexplicable and can only be understood by those who have personally experienced them in depth.

○ 커피, 차를 끓이다　**brew tea or coffee**
커피 한 주전자 끓일게요.　I will brew a pot of coffee.
자스민차 마시기를 좋아한다.　I like drinking jasmine tea.

○ 그래요? 그런가요?　**Does it? Is it?**　(앞서 나온 동사에 따라 do(es), is(are)를 선택 사용)
동의어　Is that so? Do you think so? Really?

○ ~이 틀림없다. 장담하다.　**I'm sure ~, I'm certain ~**
그 사람이 맞음에 틀림없다.　I'm certain he is right.
내일 눈이 올 것임에 틀림없다.　I'm sure it will snow tomorrow.

○ 다구　**tea utensils**

○ 옛 속담에 따르면,　**As the old saying goes, ~**
격언　**dictum**　/　속담　**proverb, old saying**
빈 수레가 요란하다.　A barking dog never bites.
서당개 삼 년이면 풍월을 읊는다.　A saint's maid quotes Latin.
만족하는 사람은 언제나 부자다.　A contented man is always rich.

○ ~의 범주에 들다　**fall under ~**
하늘, 에메랄드, 연두, 초록 색은 큰 범주에서는 '파란색'에 속한다.
The colors sky blue, emerald, green and light green all fall under "blue color" in a larger context.

○ ~하는 사람들(어떤 한 부류의 사람들을 지칭할 때)　**those who ~**
이것은 아파트 주민만을 위해 만든 겁니다.　This is only for those who live in apartments.
매일 기도하는 사람들은 만족하는 삶을 살 가능성이 높다.
Those who pray every day are very likely to live a contented life.

Free Response

1. Do you like drinking tea?

2. What kinds of tea do you like the most?

3. How do you make the tea taste the best?

4. Do you know any proverb that is related to or originated from Buddhism?

⑤ 승가대학

잭: 스님 어디 외출하십니까?

스님: 예, 사제가 승가대학을 졸업하는 날이라 졸업식에 갑니다.

잭: 승가대학은 어떤 학교입니까?

스님: 스님들을 위한 4년제 대학교라고 할 수 있지요.

잭: 그러니까 저 같은 사람은 들어갈 수가 없군요.

스님: 예, 승가대학은 스님들에게 필요한 공부를 가르치는 곳입니다.

잭: 그럼 영어도 배우나요?

스님: 물론이지요.

Unit 5 Monastic College

Jack: Seunim, where are you heading to?

Seunim: I am off to Monastic College to watch my Dharma brother's graduation ceremony.

Jack: What is Monastic College?

Seunim: It is a four-year college for Buddhist monks and nuns.

Jack: Does it mean that people like me cannot enter?

Seunim: I am afraid not. It is a Buddhist college that teaches what monastics need to know.

Jack: Does it have an English course?

Seunim: Sure, it does.

○ 승가대학　**Monastic college**

○ ~로 향하다 ~로 향해 가다　**head to~**
학교 가자.　Let's head to school.
과일 사러 시장에 가고 있어요.　I am heading to the market to buy some fruit.

○ ~로 출발하다　**be off to~**
우리는 바다로 여름휴가를 떠납니다.　We are off to the sea for the summer holiday.
제 동생 데리러 갑니다.　I am off to pick up my sister.

○ 4년제 대학　**a four-year college**
2년제 대학　a two-year college
종합대학　university　/　단과대학　college
전문대학교　technical college, vocational college, junior college, community college
방송통신대학　open university

○ 스님들　**Buddhist monks and nuns, Buddhist monastics**

○ '아니다'의 간곡한 표현　**I am afraid not**
미안하지만, 참석 못 할 것 같아요.　I am afraid I cannot attend.
내일은 너무 바쁘네요.　I am afraid I am too busy tomorrow.
약속을 미루어야 할 것 같아요.　I am afraid I should delay our meeting.

○ ~한 것　(문장 내에서 **what** + 주어 + 동사)
동생에게 필요한 것을 사주고 싶다.　I want to buy my sister what she needs.
네 맘속에 있는 이야기를 해주세요.　Tell me what's on your mind.

Pair Work　Practice by substituting the underlined words with other proper words and phrases

Yoon:　Where are you heading to?
Dalli:　I am off to <u>Michelle's university to watch her graduation</u>. What about you?
Yoon:　I was heading <u>to the library to borrow some books</u>.
Dalli:　How about going together with me <u>to see her?</u>
Yoon:　Okay.
Dalli:　She'll be happy and surprised to see you!

재가불자들을 위한 불교대학

애나:　스님! 불교를 좀 더 잘 알고 싶으면 어디서 배우면 될까요?

스님:　대부분의 사찰에서 재가불자들을 위한 불교대학을 운영하고 있어요.

애나:　그것 참 잘됐네요.

스님:　그런데 애나는 한국어 실력이 좀더 향상되어야 그곳에서 공부할 수 있을 겁니다.

애나:　아차, 그게 걸리는군요.

　　　 보통 대학처럼 4년제인가요?

스님:　아니요, 2년제이고요,

　　　 1주일에 하루만 나가서 공부하면 됩니다.

Unit 6　**Lay Buddhist college**

Anna:　Seunim, where can I learn Buddhism if I want to study it?

Seunim:　Most temples run lay Buddhist colleges.

Anna:　That's good news!

Seunim:　But I think you have to improve your Korean first to take the course.

Anna:　Ah, that's a problem! Is it a four-year college just like ordinary ones?

Seunim:　It runs for two years and the classes are held once a week.

○ 어디서 ~할 수 있어요?　　**Where can I...?**
　　어디서 우산을 살 수 있어요?　Where can I buy an umbrella?
　　화장실은 어디에 있나요?　 Where can I find the toilet in this building?

○ 재가불자　**lay Buddhists (= lay people)**
　　재가불자들은 집에서 수행합니다.　Lay Buddhists practice at home.
　　재가불자들은 오계를 실천합니다.　Lay Buddhists keep the Five Precepts.

○ 운영하다　**run (= operate)**
　　이 식당은 북한사람이 운영합니다.　This restaurant is run by a North Korean.
　　이 단체는 사람들의 기부금에 의해 거의 운영됩니다.
　　This organization is mainly run by people's donations.

○ 운영이 지속될 경우, **run**을 사용하여 기간을 나타냄
　　이 가족은 슈퍼마켓을 50년 넘게 운영하고 있다.
　　This family has run the supermarket for over 50 years.
　　3개월, 6개월, 1년, 2년 과정의 다양한 불교대학이 있습니다.
　　There are Buddhist colleges that have curriculums for 3 months, 6 months, 1 year or 2 years.

○ 일주일에 한 번씩　**once a week (= weekly)**
　　하루에 한 번씩　once a day (= daily)
　　한 달에 한 번씩　once a month (= monthly)
　　일 년에 한 번씩　once a year (= annually)
　　나는 일주일에 한 번씩 절에서 아이들에게 영어를 가르칩니다.
　　I teach kids English at the temple once a week.

Free Response

1. Have you attended a Buddhist college before?

2. What do you learn at a Buddhist college?

3. How often do the colleges offer classes?

4. What are the similarities and differences between lay Buddhist colleges and monastic colleges for Buddhist monks?

5. Do you have any good memories from the monastic college you attended?

Part 2

Buddhist Tenets
불교 교리

Chapter 1 | **Dharma Classification and Ultimate Reality** _ 제법의 분류와 실상

Unit 1   The Five Aggregates (pañca-khandhā) 오온
Unit 2   Impermanence [Anicca] 무상
Unit 3   Suffering [Dukkha] 고
Unit 4   Non-Self [Anatta] 무아
Unit 5   The Four Noble Truths 사성제
Unit 6   The Noble Eightfold Path 팔정도
Unit 7   The Twelve Links of Dependent Arising
          (paticca-samuppada) 십이연기

Chapter 2 | **Buddhist Practices** _ 불교의 수행법

Unit 1   Meditation (Ahbhāvana) 명상
Unit 2   Samatha and Vipassana 사마타와 위빠싸나
Unit 3   Ganhwa Seon 간화선
Unit 4   Sutra Reading 간경
Unit 5   What is Yeombul? 염불
Unit 6   Types of Yeombul 염불의 종류
Unit 7   Mantra Recitation 진언

Chapter 3 | **The Way of Bodhisattvas** _ 보살의 길

Unit 1   The Four Immeasurable Minds 사무량심
Unit 2   The Four Great Vows of Bodhisattva 사홍서원
Unit 3   Who Are Bodhisattva? 보살은 누구인가?

오온

오온은 사람의 존재를 분석하여 무아를 드러내기 위한 부처님 가르침의 핵심이다. 부처님은 인간을 색, 수, 상, 행, 식이라는 5가지 요소로 구분하였다. 오온은 늘 변하는 무상(無常, anicca)한 것이기에 고(苦, dukkha)이다. 이 무상한 오온에는 자아라고 부를 것이 없다(無我, anatta). 사람은 오온이 잠시 모인 것에 불과하다. 이와 같이 인간을 구성하고 있는 5가지 요소 중 그 어느 하나도 나라고 주장할 만한 것이 없음에도 불구하고, 중생들은 그것을 '나'라고 믿고 집착한다. 이를 오취온(五取蘊)이라 한다.

색(色, rūpa) : 모양과 물질
수(受, vedana) : 느낌
상(想, saññā) : 지각작용, 개념작용
행(行, saṅkhāra) : 정신적인 형성작용, 의도
식(識, viññāṇa) : 의식

Unit 1 ## The Five Aggregates (pañca-khandhā)

The theory of the five aggregates(pañca-khandhā), is an excellent Buddhist classification system which analyzes human existence. In this system, human existence is divided into five components: form, feeling, perception, mental formations and consciousness. Because the five aggregates constantly change, they are impermanent and therefore, bring suffering. There is no "self" in these five impermanent aggregates (non-self or anatman). A human being is only a temporary composition of these five aggregates. As such, there is no single component of the five aggregates which can be claimed as "self," but sentient beings continually hold on to their belief in self. This belief comes from the five aggregates of attachment.

rūpa(色) : Form or Materiality
vedana(受) : Feeling
saññā(想) : Perception
saṅkhāra(行) : Mental formations
viññāṇa(識) : Consciousness

1. The theory of the five aggregates is an excellent Buddhist _____ system which analyzes human existence. (분류)

2. In this system, human existence is divided into five components: form, _____, _____, mental formations and consciousness. (수, 상)

3. Because the five aggregates _____ change, they are impermanent and therefore, bring suffering. (항상)

4. There is no "_____" in these five impermanent aggregates. (자아)

5. A human being is only a _____ collection of these five aggregates. (일시적인)

6. Sentient beings continually _____ _____ to their belief in self. (집착하다)

7. This belief comes from the five aggregates of _____. (오취온)

8. Mental functions which perceive an _____ through discrimination, judgment and integration. (대상)

Questions

1. What is the Buddhist classification system for analyzing human existence?

2. What are the five aggregates?

3. Why do the five aggregates bring suffering?

4. Is a human being a permanent collection of the five aggregates?

5. Can you claim your perceptions as your "self?"

② 무상 [Anicca]

무상이란 물질이든 마음이든 모든 형상 세계는 끊임없이 변화하여 영원하지 않다는 것이다. 인간이 태어나고 늙고 병들고 죽는다고 하는 사실을 나타낸다. 또한 모든 현상세계가 무상한 것은 그것들이 연기하고 있기 때문이다. 연기하고 있는 존재는 모두 영원한 것이 아니며 항상 변화하여 멈추지 않는 무상한 존재라는 것을 말한다.

> 비구들이여! 온갖 현상은 무상하여 생겨나면 없어지는 성질의 것이다. 견고하지 않고 실체가 없고 즐길 것이 못 된다. 비구들은 부지런히 정진(精進)하여 해탈을 구해야 한다.
>
> 《살발다경(薩鉢多經)》

Impermanence [Anicca]

All compounded phenomena, material or mental, are in a state of constant flux and therefore not permanent. This is referred to as "impermanence (anicca)" in Buddhism. This means that human beings are born and grow old, get sick and die. In addition, all phenomena are impermanent because all things arise, exist and cease in relation to other things. All beings in the cycle of dependent arising are impermanent and always in a state of continual change.

> "Bhikkhus! All phenomenal things are impermanent and have the nature of ceasing upon arising. Things are not solid and have no substance. There is neither ultimate dimension nor enjoyable aspects in phenomena. Thus, bhikkhus should persevere in their practice and seek liberation."
>
> - *Saptasuryoda Sutra*

Fill in the Blanks

1. All _____ _____, including materiality and the mind, are in a state of constant flux and therefore not permanent. (조합된 현상, 형성된 것)

2. This is referred to as "_____" in Buddhism. (무상)

3. This means that human beings are born and _____ _____, get sick and die. (늙다)

4. All things _____, exist and cease in relation to other things. (일어나다)

5. All beings in the cycle of _____ _____ are impermanent. (연기)

6. All phenomenal things have the nature of _____ upon arising. (소멸)

7. Things are not _____ and have no substance. (단단한)

8. There is neither _____ _____ nor enjoyable aspects in phenomena. (절대적 경지)

9. Thus, bhikkhus should _____ in their practice and seek liberation. (정진하다)

Questions

1. Are material phenomena in a state of constant flux?

2. Is the mind permanent?

3. Do things arise independent of all other things?

4. Do phenomenal things have the nature of ceasing upon arising?

5. Why did the Buddha say that bhikkhus should persevere in their practice?

③ 고 [Dukkha]

불교에서 맨 처음 직면한 문제는 인생이 괴로움[고]으로 가득 차 있다는 것이었다. 괴로움 (dukkha)이란 자기의 생각대로 되지 않는 상태를 말한다. 태어남도 괴로움이요, 늙음도 괴로움 이요, 병듦도 괴로움이요, 죽음도 괴로움이다. 이상의 생, 노, 병, 사를 4고(四苦)라고 한다. 또한 사랑하면서도 헤어져야 하는 것도 괴로움이고, 미워하면서도 만나야 하는 것도 괴로움이고, 애써 구해도 얻지 못하는 것도 괴로움이고, 집착의 대상인 오온을 나라고 집착하는 것도 괴로움이다. 이것을 앞의 것과 합쳐 8고라 한다. 고라는 명제는 '열반은 낙이다'라고 하는 어구에 상대되는 말 이다. 따라서 일체가 고라는 말은 아직 해탈을 얻지 못하여 갈애와 집착을 갖고 있는 사람들의 입 장을 나타낸 것이다.

> '모든 형성된 것은 고통이다'라고 분명한 지혜를 갖고 관할 때에 사람은 고통에서 멀리 떠 나간다. 이것이야말로 사람이 깨끗해지는 길이다.
>
> 《테라가타》 677

Unit 3 Suffering [Dukkha]

The first problem Buddha realized was that life is full of suffering. Suffering (dukkha) is any state wherein things do not go as one wants or expects. Birth is suffering, and so is ageing. Sickness is suffering, and so is death. These four things (birth, ageing, sickness and death) are referred to as the four kinds of suffering. In addition, separation from that which we love is suffering and so is association with that which we hate. Inability to fulfill our desires is suffering and so is attachment to the five aggregates by regarding them as our "self." These four kinds of psychological suffering, together with the aforementioned four, are called the eight kinds of suffering. The saying "Nirvana is bliss" is the counterpart to the saying "All formation is suffering" which is the state of those people who have not attained liberation and are dominated by craving and attachment.

Penetrating with clear insight that All compound phenomena are suffering You leave suffering far behind.

This is the way human beings become pure.

-Theragatha 677

Fill in the Blanks

1. The first problem Buddha _____ was that life is full of suffering. (깨닫다)

2. Suffering is any state wherein things do not go as one wants or _____. (기대하다)

3. Birth is suffering, and so is _____. (늙는 것)

4. Sickness is suffering, and so is _____. (죽음)

5. In addition, _____ from that which we love is suffering. (헤어짐)

6. _____ with that which we hate is suffering. (유대)

7. Inability to _____ our desires is suffering. (충족시키다)

8. _____ _____ is suffering. (일체)

9. _____ is bliss. (열반)

10. People who are dominated by _____ and attachment. (갈애)

Questions

1. What was the first problem the Buddha realized?

2. When things do not go as we want, is it suffering?

3. What are the four kinds of suffering?

4. Is separation from that which we love a component of the eight kinds of suffering?

5. Are non-liberated people dominated by craving?

무아 [Anatta]

'무아'라는 말은 '내가 아닌 것' 또는 '나를 갖지 않는 것'이라는 의미이다. '어떤 사물이 실체적 자아를 갖지 않은 것'이라는 뜻으로 쓰이기도 한다. 무아설은 무엇보다 먼저 '내 것이다', '자신의 소유이다'라는 생각에 대한 부정이다. 무엇인가를 내 것이라 하고 자신에게 속한 것이라고 생각하는 것은 나에 대한 망집(妄執)으로, 수행자는 먼저 이 같은 아집을 없애지 않으면 안 된다. 무엇인가를 '자신의 것이다'라고 보는 견해는 일체의 사실을 잘못 파악하는 방식으로, 진실로 자신의 것이라고 할 수 있는 바는 어떠한 것도 존재하지 않는다. 그러므로 제법무아는 이 세상에 존재하는 모든 사물은 인연으로 생겼으며, 변하지 않는 참다운 자아의 실체는 존재하지 않는다는 말이다.

> 색수상행식[五蘊]은 무상하다. 그리고 무상한 것은 고이다. 고인 것은 무아이다. 무아인 것은, 그것은 내것이 아니고, 이것은 내가 아니고, 나의 자아가 아니다'라고 이와 같이 이것을 있는 그대로 바른 지혜로 보아야 한다. 《맛지마니까야》

Non-Self [Anatta]

"Non-self" means "that which is not the self," or "that which does not have a self." It can also mean that "things do not have an inherent substantial self." The theory of non-self negates all thoughts of "me, my, or mine." To think that something is "mine" or belongs to "me" is a deluded attachment to the self. Practitioners must extinguish these kinds of deluded attachments above all else. To regard something as "one's own" is a wrong perception. In fact, there is nothing that can be regarded as one's own. Therefore, the exposition "All things lack inherent existence" means that all things in the world have arisen dependent upon causes and conditions and that there is no true substance of self which does not change.

"Form, feeling, perception, mental formations and consciousness are all impermanent. And what is impermanent is suffering. What is suffering is non-self. What is non-self is to see things as they are with correct wisdom by realizing, "This is not mine, this is not me, and this is not my self."

-Majjhima Nikàya

Fill in the Blanks

1. "Non-self" means "that which is not the _____." (자아)

2. It can also mean that "things do not have an inherent _____ self." (실체적인)

3. The theory of non-self _____ all thoughts of "me, my, or mine." (부정하다)

4. To think that something is "mine" is a _____ _____ to the self. (망집)

5. _____ must extinguish these kinds of deluded attachments. (수행자들)

6. To regard something as "one's own" is a _____ perception. (잘못된)

7. In fact, there is nothing that can be _____ as one's own. (여기다)

8. All things in the world have arisen dependent upon _____ and _____. (원인, 조건)

9. There is no true _____ of self which does not change. (실체)

10. "Form, feeling, perception, mental formations and _____ are all impermanent. (식)

11. What is impermanent is _____. (고)

12. What is suffering is _____. (무아)

13. What is non-self is to see things as they are with _____ _____. (바른 지혜)

Questions

1. What does the theory of non-self negate?

2. What must practitioners extinguish above all else?

3. Is regarding something as your own wrong perception?

4. Is there any true substance of self which does not change?

5. If you understand the concept of non-self, would you say "this is mine and this is me?"

⑤ 사성제

사성제는 붓다가 정각을 이룬 뒤 다섯 비구에게 행한 최초의 설법이다. 사성제는 괴로움[苦], 괴로움의 원인[集], 괴로움의 소멸[滅], 괴로움의 소멸로 이끄는 길[道]을 가리킨다. 즉 이 세계는 괴로운 것이며, 그 괴로움의 원인은 갈애와 욕망이 있기 때문이다. 따라서 그 괴로움을 소멸하려면 팔정도를 행하여 갈애를 제거하지 않으면 안 된다는 가르침이 바로 사성제이다. 사성제를 통해 인생의 괴로움 전반에 대한 확실한 통찰이 있어야 진정한 수행이 시작되고 괴로움도 제거할 수 있다. 이 사성제는 부처님 가르침의 기본이며 불교의 인생관과 세계관을 설명하는 중요한 가르침이기도 하다.

> 부처님과 가르침과 승가에 귀의한 사람은, 바른 지혜로써 네 가지 거룩한 진리를 본다.
> (그것은) 괴로움, 괴로움의 근원, 괴로움의 극복, 괴로움의 소멸로 이끄는 여덟 가지 거룩한 길이다. 《법구경》 190~191

Unit 5 The Four Noble Truths

After the Buddha attained enlightenment, the Four Noble Truths constitute the first teaching he gave to the five ascetics with whom he used to practice. The Four Noble Truths are: the existence of suffering, the cause of suffering, the cessation of suffering and the path to the cessation of suffering. That is, this world is suffering, and the cause of suffering lies in our cravings and worldly desires. Thus, in order to end suffering, one must remove craving by practicing the Noble Eightfold Path. When one establishes a solid insight into all the suffering humans create, one can embark on genuine practice and overcome suffering. The Four Noble Truths are the foundation of the Buddha's teachings. They are also important as they explain the Buddhist view on life and the world.

"He, who has taken refuge in the Buddha, the Dharma and the

Sangha, penetrates with right wisdom the Four Noble Truths —
suffering, the cause of suffering, the cessation of suffering, and the
Noble Eightfold Path leading to the cessation of suffering."

-*Dhammapada* 190~191

Fill in the Blanks

1. The Four Noble Truths constitute the first teaching he gave to the five _____.
   (사문 또는 고행수행자)

2. The Four Noble Truths are: the _____ of suffering, the _____ of suffering,
   the cessation of suffering and the path to the cessation of suffering. (존재, 원인)

3. The cause of suffering lies in our cravings and _____ _____. (세속적 욕망)

4. Thus, in order to end suffering, one must _____ craving. (없애다)

5. When one establishes a solid insight into all the suffering humans _____,
   (만들어내다)

6. One can _____ _____ genuine practice and overcome suffering. (시작하다)

7. The Four Noble Truths are the _____ of the Buddha's teachings. (기본)

8. "He, who has taken _____ in the Buddha, the Dharma and the Sangha, penetrates
   with right wisdom the Four Noble Truths. (귀의)

Questions

1. What was the first teaching the Buddha gave to the five ascetics?

2. What is the cause of suffering?

3. What must you do to end suffering?

4. Are the Four Noble Truths the foundation of the Buddha's teachings?

5. What explains the Buddhist view on life?

⑥ 팔정도

번뇌와 괴로움를 제거하고 열반의 경지에 이르기 위한 8가지 실천 항목으로, 다음과 같다.

① 올바른 이해(正見)

사물을 있는 그대로 이해하는 것이다. 결국 사성제의 이해를 말한다.

② 올바른 생각(正思惟)

모든 존재에 확산될 수 있는 사심 없는 이욕(離慾)의 사유, 사랑과 비폭력의 사유를 의미한다.

③ 올바른 언어(正語)

일상적 언어생활에서 볼 때 거짓된[妄語], 험담이나 욕설[惡口], 이간하는 말[兩舌],
쓸데없는 말[綺語] 등 4가지를 떠나는 말이다.

④ 올바른 행위(正業)

도덕적이며 올바른 신체적 행위로써 살생, 도둑질, 사음을 떠나는 것이다.

⑤ 올바른 생활(正命)

남에게 해를 끼치는 직업을 삼가고, 도덕적인 삶을 살 수 있는 직업에 의해 사는 것이다.

⑥ 올바른 노력(正精進)

마음속에 이미 일어난 해로운 법을 버리려는 노력과 아직 일어나지 않은 해로운 법을 일어
나지 않게 하려는 노력, 그리고 아직 일어나지 않은 유익한 법을 일어나게 하려는 노력과
이미 일어난 유익한 법을 지속시키려는 노력이다.

⑦ 올바른 마음챙김(正念)

올바른 마음챙김으로, 올바른 생각 내지 올바른 선정을 실천하기 위해 자기 자신이나 주위의
사물을 올바로 알고 올바로 유의하는 것을 의미한다.

⑧ 올바른 집중(正定)

바른집중은 수행자의 마음에 장애가 사라졌을 때 얻어진다. 올바른 이해, 올바른 언어,
올바른 생활 등은 모두 바른 정신 집중에 의해서 비로소 완전하게 수행될 수 있다.

The Noble Eightfold Path

The Noble Eightfold Path lists the eight practices we must perfect in order
to remove afflictions and suffering and to attain nirvana.

① **Right View (Samma-ditthi):**
   To understand things as they are. Ultimately it refers to the understanding of the
   Four Noble Truths.

② **Right Thought (Samma-sankappa):**
   Selfless thought transcending personal desires, which can be extended to all beings.
   To have thoughts of love and non-violence.

③ **Right Speech (Samma-vaca):**
   In daily life, speaking without doing these four things: lying, spreading rumors or
   slandering, fomenting problems between others, and pointless chattering.

④ **Right Action (Samma-kanmmanta):**
   To act in right and ethical ways. That is, to refrain from killing, stealing, intoxicants
   and sexual misconduct.

⑤ **Right Livelihood (Samma-ajiva):**
   To make a living not from jobs which may cause harm to others, but from jobs
   which are honorable and respectable.

⑥ **Right Effort (Samma-vayama):**
   The effort to abandon unwholesome states that have already arisen and to prevent
   the arising of unarisen unwholesome states; and the effort to arouse wholesome
   states that have not yet arisen and to maintain and perfect wholesome states that
   have already arisen.

⑦ **Right Mindfulness (Samma-sati):**
   It means to become fully aware of oneself and one's surroundings with right
   mindfulness in order to practice Right Thought and Right Concentration.

⑧ **Right Concentration (Samma-samadhi):**
   Right Concentration provides a foundation for the perfect practice of Right View,
   Right Speech and Right Livelihood.

1. The Noble Eightfold Path lists the eight _____ we must perfect in order to remove afflictions and suffering. (실천항목)

2. Right View is to understand things ____ _____ ____. (있는 그대로)

3. Ultimately it _____ _____ the understanding of the Four Noble Truths. (가리키다)

4. Right Thought is _____ thought transcending personal desires. (사심없는)

5. It is to have thoughts of love and _____. (비폭력)

6. Right Speech is to speak without _____, spreading rumors or slandering, fomenting problems between others, and pointless chattering. (거짓말)

7. Right Action is to act in right and _____ ways. (도덕적인)

8. That is, to _____ _____ killing, stealing, intoxicants and sexual misconduct. (삼가다)

9. Right Livelihood is not to make a living from jobs which may cause _____ to others. (해악)

10. Right Mindfulness means to become fully _____ of oneself and one's surroundings. (알아차리다)

11. Right Concentration provides a _____ for the perfect practice of Right View. (기반)

1. If you understand things as they are, do you have Right View?
2. What is Right Thought?
3. If you spread rumors, do you practice Right Speech?
4. If you take intoxicants, do you practice Right Action?
5. If your job brings harm to others, do you practice Right Livelihood?
6. What is Right Mindfulness?

마음이 없어서 얻을 것도 없으니

마음이 없어서 얻을 것도 없으니
얻은 것이 있다면 법이라 할 수 없네
마음이 마음 아닌 줄 깨달으면
비로소 마음과 마음의 법을 알리라.

_미차가

*There is no mind and
nothing to be attained*

There is no mind and nothing to be attained.
If you say you have attained it, that it is not called Dharma.
If you realize the mind is not mind,
For the first time you understand the mind and mind-Dharma.

_By Ven. Miccika

⑦ 십이연기

모든 존재는 그것을 형성시키는 원인과 조건에 의해서 존재하기도 하고 소멸하기도 한다. 또한 상호관계에 의해서만 존재하기도 하고 소멸하기도 한다. 이것은 연기법에 대한 설명이다. 인연에 의해서 그와 같은 모습으로 성립되어 있을 뿐 독립하여 스스로 존재하는 것은 아무것도 없다. 특히 십이연기는 인간의 고통이 발생하는 원인과 과정 그리고 고통이 소멸하는 원인과 과정을 설명하는 가르침이다.

① **무명(無名)** : 사성제 등의 진리를 모르는 근본 무지를 말한다.
② **행(行)** : 무명으로부터 다음의 의식 및 의지 작용을 일으키는 것으로, 우리가 짓는 업을 뜻한다.
③ **식(識)** : 눈, 귀, 코, 혀, 몸, 뜻의 6식이다.
④ **명색(名色)** : 이름만 있고 형상이 없는 마음을 명(名)이라 하고, 이름도 있고 형체도 있는 물질을 색(色)이라 한다.
⑤ **육입(六入)** : 눈, 귀, 코, 혀, 몸, 뜻 등의 6근이다.
⑥ **촉(觸)** : 근, 경, 식이 만나서 생겨난 접촉이다.
⑦ **수(受)** : 괴로움, 즐거움, 괴로움도 아니고 즐거움도 아닌 중성의 느낌을 말한다.
⑧ **애(愛)** : 욕망의 만족을 바라는 욕구와 갈애이다.
⑨ **취(取)** : 갈애가 발전하여 자아 관념이 견고해진 것을 말한다.
⑩ **유(有)** : 생사윤회하는 중생의 업식을 말한다.
⑪ **생(生)** : 중생이 어떤 부류의 중생계에 태어나는 것을 말한다.
⑫ **노사(老死)** : 태어나서 늙고 죽는 것으로서 중생의 모든 고통을 대표한다.

Unit 7

The Twelve Links of Dependent Arising (paticca-samuppada)

All beings come into being or cease to be based on the causes and conditions which brought them into existence. In other words, they arise or cease only through interdependent relationships. This is the principle of dependent arising. Things exist as they are because of the phenomenon of causation. Nothing exists on its own independent of anything else. Dependent arising clarifies phenomenal existence and its formation.

Especially, the twelve links of dependent arising explain the causes and processes of the arising and cessation of suffering.

① **Ignorance (avijjā):** A fundamental delusion which does not know the truth, including the Four Noble Truths.

② **Mental formations (sankhāra):** Intentional actions due to ignorance; from this comes the karma we create.

③ **Consciousness (viññana):** The six consciousnesses which are: visual, auditory, olfactory, taste, tactile and conceptual consciousnesses.

④ **Name and form (nāma-rūpa):** "Name" refers to mind which has name but no form while "form" refers to the material and physical which have form.

⑤ **The six sensory gates (salāyatana):** The eyes, ears, nose, tongue, skin and mind.

⑥ **Contact (phassa):** This arises when there is interaction between the six sense organs, the objects they perceive and the six consciousnesses.

⑦ **Feeling (vedanā):** There are three types of feeling: pleasant, painful and neutral which is neither pleasant nor painful.

⑧ **Craving (tanhā):** Drives, longings and cravings that seek to satisfy desires.

⑨ **Clinging (upādāna):** It refers to a more concrete concept of self which occurs as one's cravings increase.

⑩ **Becoming (bhava):** The karmic consciousness of sentient beings in cyclic existence.

⑪ **Birth (jāti):** The entrance of a sentient being into the realm of sentient beings.

⑫ **Ageing and death (jarā-marana):** Birth, sickness, ageing and death represent the suffering of sentient beings.

1. All beings come into being or cease to be based on the causes and conditions which brought them into _____. (존재)

2. In other words, they arise or cease only through _____ relationships. (상호의존적인)

3. Nothing exists on its own _____ _____ anything else. (독립하여)

4. Dependent arising _____ phenomenal existence and its formation. (밝혀주다)

5. Because twelve phases interact with each other in the process of _____, Buddhists call them the "twelve links of dependent arising." (인연)

6. Ignorance is a fundamental _____ which does not know the truth. (미망)

7. Mental formations are _____ actions due to ignorance. (의지적)

8. The six consciousnesses which are: _____, auditory, _____, taste, tactile and conceptual consciousnesses. (시각, 후각)

9. "Name" refers to mind which has name but no _____. (형태)

10. The six sensory gates are the eyes, ears, nose, _____, skin and mind. (혀)

11. Craving is drives and longings that seek to _____ desires. (만족시키다)

12. Birth, sickness, ageing and death _____ the suffering of sentient beings. (대표하다)

1. Do things arise or cease through interdependent relationships?

2. How many phases or links are there in dependent arising?

3. What is a fundamental delusion which does not know the truth?

4. Do intentional actions originating from ignorance create karma?

5. What are the six sensory gates?

6. Which interaction brings you feelings of suffering or pleasure?

7. What arises dependent upon clinging?

때가 낀 옷을 빨듯이 공부를 해야 한다

때가 낀 옷을 빨듯이 공부를 해야 한다
옷은 본래부터 있었던 것이고
때는 밖에서부터 온 것이다
보고 들은 일체의 유무와 소리나 형상에 관한 말씀은
마치 기름때와도 같으니
절대로 마음이 머물게 하지 말라.

_백장 선사

Studying is like washing dirty clothes

Studying is like washing dirty clothes.
The clothes are basically existent,
the dirt has come from outside.
Listening to words that say all existence and
 non-existence, sound and matter, is
just like the dirt and grease.
Do not have the mind rest with them in the least.

_By Ven. Baizhang

① 명상

불교에서 명상이란 깨달음을 얻기 위해 마음을 안으로 돌려 다스리는 것을 말한다. 부처님과 조사들은 여러 가지 명상법을 가르쳤다. 명상은 행·주·좌·와 어느 때라도 할 수 있지만 가장 강조되는 것은 앉아서 하는 좌선이다. 명상에 들어가기 전 부처님의 가르침을 바르게 이해하고 정해진 계율을 잘 지키는 도덕적인 삶이 요구된다. 부처님은 명상 수행을 잘하면 두 가지를 계발할 수 있으니, 첫째는 마음을 안정시키고 집중하게 해주는 '고요함'(사마타)이고 둘째는 형성된 것을 보고 통찰력(위빠사나)를 얻게 된다고 하셨다.

Unit 1 Meditation (bhāvana)

In Buddhism, meditation means to turn one's mind inward and pacify it. Buddhists practice meditation to attain enlightenment. The Buddha and the patriarchs taught various kinds of meditation. Meditation can be practiced any time and any place whether one is walking, standing, sitting or lying down. However, it is the sitting meditation that is emphasized most in Buddhism. A prerequisite to meditation practice is to fully understand the Buddha's teachings and to live an ethical life by observing the prescribed precepts.

The Buddha said one can develop two qualities through consistent meditation, those being: "calm-abiding" (samatha) which helps keep the mind calm and concentrated; and "insight" (vipassana) through which one may penetrate one's own mental fabrications.

1. In Buddhism, meditation means to turn one's mind _____ and pacify it. (안으로)

2. Buddhists practice meditation to _____ enlightenment. (얻다)

3. The Buddha and the _____ taught various kinds of meditation. (조사들)

4. Meditation can be practiced any time and any place whether one is _____,

   _____, _____ or _____. (행 주 좌 와)

5. However, it is the _____ _____ that is emphasized most in Buddhism. (좌선)

6. The Buddha said one can develop two _____ through consistent meditation. (자질)

7. Calm-abiding or _____ helps keep the mind calm and concentrated. (사마타)

8. Insight or _____ helps one to penetrate one's own mental fabrications. (위빠사나)

Questions

1. What does meditation mean to Buddhists?

2. Why do Buddhists practice meditation?

3. Can meditation be practiced only in Seon halls?

4. Can you practice meditation while walking?

5. What type of meditation is most emphasized in Buddhism?

6. What are the two qualities one can develop through consistent meditation?

사마타와 위빠사나

사마타는 집중명상, 또는 '고요히 머무는' 명상이라 불린다. 위빠사나는 통찰명상이라고 불린다. 사마타는 마음을 고요히 하여 한곳에 집중하도록 해준다. 위빠사나는 사마타 명상의 적정 속에서 정신과 물질의 무상성과 연기성을 깨닫는 것이다.

부처님은 사마타와 위빠사나에 대해 다음과 같이 말씀하셨다.

> 비구들이여, 사마타를 닦으면 어떤 이로움을 경험하는가? 마음이 계발된다. 마음이 계발되면 어떤 이로움을 경험하는가? 욕망이 제거된다.
>
> 비구들이여, 위빠사나를 닦으면 어떤 이로움을 경험하는가? 통찰지가 계발된다. 통찰지가 계발되면 어떤 이로움을 경험하는가? 무명이 제거된다.
>
> 《영지(靈知)의 일부 경》(AN 2.3.10)

Samatha and Vipassana

Samatha meditation is called "concentration meditation" or "calm-abiding meditation." Vipassana meditation is called "insight meditation." Samatha meditation helps to calm one's mind and concentrate it on a single object. Based on the tranquility one has attained through samatha meditation, one practices vipassana meditation to realize the impermanence and interdependence of mind and materiality. About samatha and vipassana, the Buddha said:

> "Bhikkhus, when samatha is cultivated, what benefit does it bring?
> The mind is developed.
> When the mind is developed, what benefit does it bring?
> All craving is extinguished.
> Bhikkhus, when vipassana is cultivated, what benefit does it bring?
> Insight is developed.
> When insight is developed, what benefit does it bring?
> All ignorance is extinguished."
>
> - *Vijjabhagiya-sutta* (AN 2.3.10)

1. Samatha meditation is called "_____ meditation" or "_____ meditation."
   (집중, 고요히 머무는)

2. Vipassana meditation is called "_____ meditation." (통찰)

3. Samatha meditation helps to concentrate one's mind on a single _____. (대상)

4. Through samatha meditation one attains _____. (적정)

5. One practices vipassana meditation to realize the _____ and _____ of
   mind and materiality. (무상성, 연기성)

6. When samatha is cultivated, the mind is _____. (개발된다)

7. When the mind is developed, what _____ does it bring? (이로움)

8. When vipassana is cultivated, _____ is developed. (통찰력)

9. When insight is developed, all _____ is extinguished.(무지)

Questions

1. Does "calm-abiding meditation" refer to samatha meditation?

2. What is vipassana meditation alternatively called?

3. Does samatha meditation use a single object of meditation?

4. Does vipassana meditation help one to realize impermanence?

5. When samatha is cultivated, what benefit does it bring?

6. When the mind is developed, what benefit does it bring?

7. When vipassana is cultivated, what benefit does it bring?

8. When insight is developed, what benefit does it bring?

간화선

간화선(看話禪)이란 화두(話頭)를 참구하여 본래 성품을 바로 보는 참선법이다. 화두란 부처님과 조사 스님들이 하신 말씀 중에서 언어의 길과 생각의 길이 닿지 않는 말이다. 수행자는 이 말과 생각으로는 알 수 없는 화두에 의심을 하기 시작하여 마침내 온 마음이 화두와 하나가 되어 그 의심을 타파하게 된다. 간화선은 또한 화두를 참구하여 깨치는 수행법이라 하여 화두선(話頭禪)이라고도 한다.

Unit 3 Ganhwa Seon

Ganhwa Seon refers to a Seon (Ch. Chan/ Jap. Zen) meditation which guides practitioners to see directly their true nature through the observance of a hwadu (Ch. huatou/ Jap. koan). A hwadu is a phrase uttered by the Buddha or the patriarchs to which the paths of words and thoughts are severed. Practitioners begin to arouse doubt on the hwadu which can not be resolved through language or thought. Eventually, they become one with the hwadu, penetrating the doubt. Ganhwa Seon is also referred to as "Hwadu Seon" as it is a practice to attain awakening by working on a hwadu.

1. Ganhwa Seon guides practitioners to see directly their _____ _____. (참성품)

2. Ganhwa Seon practitioners _____ a hwadu. (참구하다)

3. A hwadu is a phrase _____ by the Buddha or the patriarchs. (말하다)

4. A hwadu is a phrase to which the _____ of words and thoughts are severed. (길)

5. Practitioners begin to arouse _____ on the hwadu. (의심)

6. The hwadu which can not be resolved through language or _____. (생각)

7. Eventually, they become one with the hwadu, _____ the doubt. (타파하다)

8. Ganhwa Seon is also referred to as "_____ _____." (화두선)

Questions

1. What does Ganhwa Seon guide practitioners to see directly?

2. What does Ganhwa Seon use to guide practitioners to enlightenment?

3. Why is Ganhwa Seon also referred to as "Hwadu Seon?"

4. Who uttered the words which constitute a hwadu?

5. In observing a hwadu, can one use the path of language?

6. Does arousing doubt facilitate the breakthrough of a hwadu?

④ 간경

간경은 경전을 독송하는 수행이다. 경전은 부처님의 가르침을 기록한 것으로 불교에서는 보통 법보(法寶)라 한다. 대승경전에서는 경을 받아지니고 독송하며 남에게 설해주는 공덕에 대하여 찬탄하고 있다. 간경에는 소리를 내어 경전을 읽는 것은 물론 소리 없이 마음속으로 읽는 경우도 포함된다. 경전을 읽는 순간은 나와 부처님이 함께하는 시간이다. 마치 부처님이 내 앞에서 그 경전을 설하고 있고 내가 그 말씀을 직접 듣고 있다는 마음으로 경을 읽고 가르침의 뜻을 음미한다. 경전의 말씀이 몸과 마음에 체화되면 일상에서 가르침대로 행할 수가 있게 된다.

Unit 4 Sutra Reading

Buddhist sutras are the records of the Buddha's teachings. Buddhism refers to sutras as the Dharma Jewel and reveres them as objects of faith. In addition, all Mahayana sutras praise the merits of receiving and reciting the sutras as well as teaching them to others. Sutra reading includes reading the scriptures either quietly or aloud.

When reading sutras, we are communing with the Buddha. We should read the sutra and appreciate the inner meaning of the teaching as if the Buddha was teaching the sutra in front of us and we were listening to him in person. When the words of the sutra become embodied within our whole being, we can conduct our daily lives according to the Buddha's teachings.

1. Buddhist sutras are the _____ of the Buddha's teachings. (기록)

2. Buddhism refers to sutras as the _____ _____. (법보)

3. Buddhism _____ sutras as objects of faith. (숭배하다, 받들다)

4. Mahayana sutras praise the _____ of receiving and reciting the sutras. (공덕)

5. Sutra reading includes reading the scriptures either quietly or _____. (소리 내어)

6. When reading sutras, we are _____ with the Buddha. (함께하다, 교감하다)

7. We should read the sutra and _____ the inner meaning of the teaching. (음미하다)

8. As if we were listening to the Buddha _____ _____. (직접)

9. We can conduct our daily lives _____ ____ the Buddha's teachings. (따라서)

Questions

1. Do Buddhist sutras contain the Buddha's teachings?

2. Why does Buddhism revere sutras?

3. Does sutra reading include reading the scriptures quietly?

4. Do you read sutras every day?

5. Do you have any favorite sutras?

6. How can we embody the words of the sutra in our daily lives?

7. Do you like to read sutras quietly or aloud?

⑤ 염불

염불은 부처님을 마음속으로 간절히 생각하며 부처님의 명호를 송하는 것이다. 예를 들어 아미타불 염불을 할 경우 '나무아미타불'을 집중하여 되풀이 염송하는 것이다. 염불은 누구나 쉽게 할 수 있는 수행법이며 참회를 하면서 동시에 공덕을 지을 수 있는 수행법이다. 아울러 아미타불의 본원력에 의지하여 가장 빠르게 정토왕생을 할 수 있는 수행법이기도 하다. 염불은 불보살의 본원력에 의지한다는 측면에서는 타력수행법이지만 스스로가 염불을 해야 하고 원력을 세워야 하므로 자력수행법으로도 볼 수 있다.

Unit 5 ## What is Yeombul?

Yeombul or "recitation of the names of the buddhas" is to chant the name of a specific buddha while single-mindedly thinking of him with one's whole being. For example, in the case of the buddha known as Amitabha, one concentrates fully on him while repeatedly chanting "Namu Amitabul" or "Homage to Amitabha Buddha."

Yeombul is a practice most people can do without much difficulty. While practicing Yeombul, one can repent as well as accumulate merits. Furthermore, Yeombul is the most expedient way to be reborn in the Pure Land by relying on the vows of the buddhas and bodhisattvas.

Yeombul is an "other-power practice" in that it relies on the power of vows made by buddhas and bodhisattvas. However, Yeombul is also a "self-power practice" in that one practices it on one's own while making one's own vows.

1. Yeombul is to _____ the name of a specific buddha. (송하다)

2. When chanting Amitabha, practitioners _____ think of Amitabha. (일심으로)

3. "Namu Amitabul" means "_____ to Amitabha Buddha." (귀의)

4. Yeombul is a practice most people can do without much _____. (어려움)

5. While practicing Yeombul, one can _____ as well as accumulate merits. (참회하다)

6. Yeombul is the most expedient way to be reborn in the _____ _____. (정토)

7. Yeombul is an "other-power practice" in that it relies on the power of _____ made by buddhas and bodhisattvas. (서원)

8. Yeombul is also a "_____ practice" in that one practices it on one's own while making one's own vows. (자력)

Questions

1. In yeombul, does one chant the name of a specific buddha or bodhisattva?

2. What does "Namu Amitabul" mean?

3. Is yeombul a difficult practice not easily accessible to the public?

4. While practicing yeombul, can you repent your wrongdoings?

5. Is yeombul an "other-power practice?"

염불의 종류

염불의 종류는 크게 두 가지로 나눌 수 있다. 첫째, 칭명염불은 '관세음보살'처럼 불보살의 명호를 부르거나 '나무아미타불'처럼 불보살에게 귀의를 표하는 것이다.

둘째, 관상염불은 불보살의 특징이나 모습을 관하는 것과 부처님의 수승한 공덕이나 극락세계의 여러 장엄한 모습을 마음속으로 떠올리면서 명호를 외우는 것이다.

Types of Yeombul

Yeombul or "recitation of the names of the buddhas" can be practiced in two ways. The first way is to recite the names of buddhas and bodhisattvas such as Gwanseumbosal or Avalokitesvara, or declare homage to them, as in "Namu Amitabul" ("Homage to Amitabha Buddha").

The second way is to recite the names of buddhas and bodhisattvas while contemplating their features or images as well as contemplating their excellent merits and the magnificent features of the Pure Land.

Fill in the Blanks

1. Yeombul can be practiced in two _____. (방식)

2. The first way is to _____ the names of buddhas. (염송하다)

3. It is to declare _____ to them, as in "Namu Amitabul." (귀의)

4. Recite the names while contemplating their excellent _____. (공덕)

5. Recite the names while contemplating the magnificent _____ of the Pure Land.(특징)

1. Is "Namu Amitabul" declaring homage to Amitabha Buddha?

2. When practicing yeombul, do you recite the names of the buddha or bodhisattva absent-mindedly?

3. When practicing yeombul, do you sometimes visualize the magnificent Pure Land?

진언

진언은 일종의 주문으로, 부처님의 비밀스러운 말 또는 진실한 말을 의미한다.

말에는 오묘한 힘이 있다. 마음을 전달하는 말의 의미는 곧 강력한 힘을 발휘하게 된다. 진언이란 부처님의 서원과 여러 보살의 서원이 응집된 소리로, 초월적이고 신성하고 신비한 힘이 담겨져 있다. 수행자는 진언을 외움으로써 신비한 능력을 갖추게 되고 결국 깨달음에 이르게 된다. 그래서 진언은 우리말로 해석하지 않음을 원칙으로 하고 있다.

한국에서 수행하는 대표적인 진언은 주로 천수다라니와 능엄주 및 육자대명왕진언, 광명진언 등이 해당한다. 진언을 외울 때는 무조건 외우는 게 아니라 불보살의 대자대비한 마음을 가슴 깊이 새기면서 암송해야 한다

Mantra Recitation

A mantra or a short dharani (dhāraṇī) is a mystical utterance. They are the esoteric words or true words of the Buddha.

Words contain mysterious power. When words properly convey the human mind, they can exert strong power.

Within a mantra the vows of the buddhas and bodhisattvas are condensed. Thus, mantras have transcendental, sacred and mysterious powers. By reciting mantras, practitioners can attain mysterious powers, which will eventually lead them to buddhahood. That's why, in principle, mantras can not be perfectly translated into any language.

Some outstanding mantras practiced in Korea are: the Thousand Hands Dharani, the Surangama Dharani, the Six-Syllable Mantra of the Great Luminous King (om mani padme hum) and the Mantra of Light (The Dharani of Vairocana Buddha).

Mantra recitation should be practiced with the right frame of mind.

One should imagine the limitless compassion of the buddhas and bodhisattvas in the depth of their hearts when reciting them.

1. A mantra or a short dhāraṇī is a _____ utterance. (신비로운)

2. Mantras are the _____ words or true words of the Buddha. (비밀스러운)

3. When words properly convey the human mind, they can _____ strong power. (발하다)

4. Within a mantra the _____ of the buddhas and bodhisattvas are condensed. (서원들)

5. Thus, mantras have _____, sacred and mysterious powers. (초월적인)

6. That's why, ___ _____, mantras can not be perfectly translated into any language.
   (원칙 상)

7. The Thousand _____ Dharani. (천수다라니)

8. The _____ Dharani. (능엄주)

9. The _____ Mantra of the Great Luminous King (육자대명왕진언)

10. The Mantra of _____. (광명진언)

11. Mantra recitation should be practiced with the _____ frame of mind. (바른)

1. Are mantras mystical?

2. Are mantras the exoteric words of the Buddha?

3. What are condensed in a mantra?

4. Why do mantras have power?

5. Does mantra recitation help you to attain buddhahood?

6. Can mantras be completely translated into language?

7. What are some of the popular mantras in Korea?

8. What is the right frame of mind to have when reciting a mantra?

사무량심

대승보살이 중생을 제도하기 위해 갖추고 있는 네 가지 한량없는 마음으로 자·비·희·사(慈·悲·喜·捨)를 말한다. 자무량심(慈無量心)은 일체중생을 내 몸과 같이 생각하여 항상 모든 중생에게 기쁨을 주려는 마음이다. 비무량심(悲無量心)은 모든 중생에게 고통을 없애주려는 마음이다. 희무량심(喜無量心)은 모든 중생이 기쁨을 얻게 하고 그 기쁨에 동참하는 마음이다. 사무량심(捨無量心)은 모든 중생을 절대평등하게 보고 어여삐 여기는 마음이다.

> 외아들을 보호하기 위하여 목숨을 거는 어머니처럼
> 뭇 생명을 향한 무량한 자비심을 닦아야 하나니
>
> 넓은 우주를 감싸는 마음으로 무량한 자비심을 닦아라
> 상, 하 그 어디에도 매이지 않고 미움도 악의도 넘어선 자비를.
>
> 《자비경》 Sn 143~152

The Four Immeasurable Minds

Mahayana bodhisattvas have four kinds of limitless minds to deliver sentient beings from suffering. These four minds of immeasurable concern for others are: metta, karuṇā, muditā and upekkhā.

The immeasurable mind of loving-kindness (metta) is the mind which considers all sentient beings as one's self and wants to bestow joy upon them. The immeasurable mind of compassion (karuṇā) is the mind which wants to save all beings from suffering. The immeasurable mind of joy (muditā) is the mind which wants to help all beings acquire joy and to share this joy as one's own. The immeasurable mind of equanimity (upekkhā) treats all beings equally and with compassion without distinguishing between friend and enemy.

Just as a mother would guard her only child
At the risk of her own life
Even so towards all beings
Let him cultivate boundless mind

Let thoughts of boundless love pervade the whole world
Above, below and across
Without any obstruction
Without any hatred, without any enmity

- Karaniya Metta Sutta (Sn 143-152)

Fill in the Blanks

1. Mahayana bodhisattvas have _____ _____ of limitless minds. (네 가지)

2. The four immeasurable minds have the purpose to deliver sentient beings from
   _____. (고)

3. These four _____ concern for others are: metta, karuṇā, muditā and upekṣa.
   (헤아릴 수 없는)

4. The immeasurable mind of loving-kindness (metta) wants to _____ joy and
   happiness upon all sentient beings. (주다)

5. The immeasurable mind of _____ (karuṇā) is the mind which wants to save all
   beings from suffering. (비)

6. The immeasurable mind of _____ (muditā) is the mind which wants to help all
   beings acquire happiness. (희)

7. The immeasurable mind of _____ (upekṣa) treats all beings equally and with
   compassion. (사)

8. It doesn't distinguish _____ friend and enemy. (구분하다, 가리다)

9. Just as a mother would _____ her only child (지키다)

10. Let him _____ boundless mind (닦다)

11. Let thoughts of boundless love _____ the whole world (두루 퍼지다)

12. Without any _____ (미움)

Questions

1. Why do Mahayana bodhisattvas have four kinds of limitless minds?

2. Are the four minds the minds of immeasurable loving-kindness, compassion, joy and equanimity?

3. Do bodhisattvas consider all sentient beings as one's self?

4. Does the immeasurable mind of joy become jealous when a neighbor gets rich?

5. Does the immeasurable mind of equanimity distinguish between friend and enemy?

마음의 땅에서 여러 씨앗이 자라나며

마음의 땅에서 여러 씨앗이 자라나며
현상을 말미암아 다시 이치가 자라나네
결과가 원만하면 보리도 원만하리니
꽃이 피면 세계가 일어나네.

_반야다라

The mind-ground gives birth to seeds

The mind-ground gives birth to seeds
And due to particulars further gives birth to principle
When the fruit is matured and the bodhi perfect
The flower opens and the world is produced.

_By Ven. Prajñātāra

② 사홍서원

불자로서의 삶의 목표는 보살도의 실천을 통한 행복과 해탈을 이루는 데 있다. 이러한 의미에서 불자들은 보살의 길을 가겠다는 네 가지 큰 서원을 세우는데 이를 사홍서원(四弘誓願)이라 한다. 한국에서의 모든 불교의례는 사홍서원으로 마무리된다. 이 사홍서원은 중국 천태종 남악 혜사 (C.E. 515-577) 선사의 〈입서원문〉에서 유래한다.

중생을 다 건지오리다. (중생무변서원도 衆生無邊誓願度)
번뇌를 다 끊으오리다. (번뇌무진서원단 煩惱無盡誓願斷)
법문을 다 배우리로다. (법문무량서원학 法門無量誓願學)
불도를 다 이루오리다. (불도무상서원성 佛道無上誓願成)

Unit 2 The Four Great Vows of Bodhisattva

For Buddhists, the goal of life is to attain happiness and liberation through the practice of the bodhisattva way of life. Thus, Buddhists make four great vows to declare they will walk the bodhisattva path. In Korea, all Buddhist ceremonies end with these four great vows. They originated from the *Tract on Establishing the Vow* by Nanyue Huisi (CE 515-577), the 2nd Patriarch of the Chinese Tiantai School.

Living beings are countless; I vow to take them all across.
Afflictions are inexhaustible; I vow to eliminate them all.
The teachings are immeasurable; I vow to learn them all.
The Buddha Way is unsurpassed; I vow to attain it.

1. For Buddhists, the _____ of life is to attain happiness. (목적)

2. To attain liberation through the practice of the _____ _____ of _____. (보살도)

3. Thus, Buddhists make _____ _____ _____ to declare they will walk the bodhisattva path. (사홍서원)

4. In Korea, all Buddhist ceremonies _____ with these four great vows. (끝나다)

5. They originated from the Tract on Establishing the Vow by Nanyue Huisi (CE 515-577), the 2nd _____ of the Chinese Tiantai School. (조사)

6. Living beings are _____. (무수한)

7. I vow to take them all _____. (건너게, 건너편으로)

8. _____ are inexhaustible. (번뇌)

9. I vow to _____ them all. (제거하다)

10. The _____ are immeasurable. (가르침)

11. I vow to learn to _____ them all. (들어 가다)

12. The Buddha _____ is unsurpassed. (도)

Questions

1. Why do Buddhists make four great vows?

2. Do most Mahayana Buddhists consider the bodhisattva path as their ideal?

3. What do all Buddhist ceremonies in Korea end with?

4. Where did the four great vows originate from?

5. Do you empathize with the four great vows when you take them?

보살은 누구인가?

보살 곧 보디사트바(bodhisattva)라는 말은 '깨달음을 구하는 중생'이라는 의미를 지니는데, 한마디로 보살은 '붓다의 길을 걸어가는' 사람들이다.

보살은 깨달음을 구하는 동시에(상구보리) 이웃과 더불어 아픔을 함께 나누면서 성불의 그날까지 수행해 나가는 존재이다(하화중생). 대승의 불자들은 모두가 이 보살을 실생활의 이상으로 삼고 삶을 살아간다.

경전에도 다양한 보살이 등장한다. 구도의 보살인 선재동자, 자비의 관세음보살, 지혜의 문수보살, 실천의 보현보살, 서원의 지장보살 등이 있다.

> 땅 위에 엎드린 채, 보살은 이렇게 생각했습니다.
> "원한다면 지금 당장이라도 나의 번뇌를 태워버릴 수도 있으리라.
> 그러나 여기서 내가 진리를 깨달아 홀로 저 언덕으로 건너간들 무엇하겠는가.
> 나는 모든 것을 아는 지혜를 획득하여 신들을 포함한 이 세계의 사람들 속에서
> 부처가 되리라.
> 윤회의 흐름을 끊고, 세 가지 생존(욕계,색계,무색계)을 벗어나, 진리의 배에 올라서
> 신들을 포함한 이 세계의 많은 사람들을 구제하리라."
>
> 《자타카 니다나카타》

Unit 3 Who Are Bodhisattva?

The word "bodhisattva" means "a sentient being who seeks after enlightenment." In short, bodhisattvas are those who walk "the path of buddhahood."

Bodhisattvas not only seek buddhahood but also share the suffering of their neighbors and practice with them until they attain enlightenment. Mahayana bodhisattvas live their daily lives with bodhisattvas as their ideal.

Various bodhisattvas appear in the sutras: Sudhana who seeks after truth; Avalokitesvara, the Bodhisattva of Compassion; Manjusri, the Bodhisattva of Wisdom; Samantabhadra, the Bodhisattva of Great Action; and Ksitigarbha, the Bodhisattva of Great Vows.

While prostrating on the ground, the Bodhisattva thought.

If I wanted, I could burn all my afflictions right now.

However, what good would it bring if I am awakened to the truth and cross over to the other shore alone?

I will attain omniscience and become a buddha in the midst of people in this world as well as among heavenly beings.

I will sever the cycle of samsara, extinguish the three existences in the realms of desire, form and formlessness, board the ship of truth and save all people in this world, as well as heavenly beings.

-Jātaka-nidānakathā

Fill in the Blanks

1. The word "bodhisattva" means "a sentient being who _____ _____ enlightenment." (구하다)

2. In short, bodhisattvas are those who walk "the _____ of buddhahood." (도)

3. Bodhisattvas _____ the suffering of their neighbors. (나누다)

4. Mahayana bodhisattvas live their daily lives with bodhisattvas as their _____. (이상)

5. _____ who seeks after truth. (선재)

6. Avalokitesvara, the Bodhisattva of _____. (자비)

7. _____, the Bodhisattva of Wisdom. (문수)

8. _____, the Bodhisattva of Great Action (보현)

9. _____, the Bodhisattva of Great Vows. (지장)

10. If I wanted, I could _____ all my afflictions right now. (태우다)

11. However, what _____ would it bring if I am awakened to the truth and cross over to

the other shore alone? (좋은 점, 소용)

12. I will sever the cycle of _____, (윤회)

13. I will extinguish the three existences in the realms of desire, _____and formlessness. (색계)

14. I will _____ the ship of truth. (타다)

Questions

1. What is the ideal of a Mahayana bodhisattva in daily life?

2. Do many bodhisattvas appear in the sutras?

3. Which sutra does Sudhana appear in?

4. What is Samantabhadra Bodhisattva renowned for?

5. Does a bodhisattva cross over to the other shore alone?

6. If you sever the cycle of samsara, will you be reborn?

7. Is the ship of truth also called the "wisdom dragon ship?"

작년의 가난은 가난이 아니었네

작년의 가난은 가난이 아니었네
금년의 가난이 진짜 가난일세
작년에는 송곳 꽂을 땅이 없더니
금년에는 송곳마저 없어져 버렸네.

_향엄 지한

*Last year's poverty was
not real poverty*

Last year's poverty was not real poverty
This year's poverty is real
Last year, there was no ground wherein to plunge an awl
This year, not even the awl remains.

_By Ven. Xiangyan Zhixian

Part 3

The History and Culture of Korean Buddhism

한국불교의 역사와 문화

Chapter 1 | **Buddhist Holidays** _ 불교의 명절

Unit 1 The Day the Buddha Came and
        Renunciation Day 부처님오신날, 출가재일
Unit 2 Bodhi Day and Parinirvana Day 성도재일, 열반재일

Chapter 2 | **Ceremonial Sutras and Dharma**
           Instruments _ 의식용 경전과 법구

Unit 1 The Thousand Hands Sutra and the Diamond Sutra
        천수경, 금강경
Unit 2 The Heart Sutra and the Amitabha Sutra
        반야심경, 아미타경
Unit 3 The Four Dharma Instruments 사물
Unit 4 The Moktak and the Seon Stick 목탁, 죽비
Unit 5 Monastic Robes: Gasa and Jangsam 가사, 장삼

Chapter 3 | **Temple Architecture** _ 사찰건축

Unit 1 The One Pillar Gate and the Gate of Non-Duality
        일주문, 불이문
Unit 2 The Diamond Gate and the Gate of Heavenly Kings
        금강문, 천왕문
Unit 3 Buddhist Painting 불화
Unit 4 Stupas and Seungtaps (Monks' Stupa) 탑, 승탑
Unit 5 Stone Lanterns and Wind Bells 석등, 풍경

Chapter 4 | **Buddhist Cultural Heritage of Korea** _
           우리 불교문화유산

Unit 1 The Tripitaka Koreana and the Janggyeong Panjeon
        at Haein-sa Temple 해인사의 팔만대장경과 장경판전
Unit 2 Gyeongju's Bulguk-sa Temple and Seokguram Grotto
        경주의 불국사와 석굴암
Unit 3 The Lotus Lantern Festival 연등축제

❶ 부처님오신날, 출가재일

불교의 4대 명절은 부처님오신날, 출가재일, 성도재일, 열반재일이다. '부처님오신날'은 싯다르타 태자가 탄생한 날로, 음력 4월 8일이다. 부처님은 무수한 생 동안에 보살행의 과정을 거쳐 당신의 의지대로 이 세상에 오셨기에 일반적으로 영어로는 '부처님탄신일'이라고 부르지만, 한국 불자들은 주로 '부처님오신날'이라고 부른다. 불교의 행사 가운데 가장 큰 명절로 부처님의 탄생을 축하하고 기념하는 봉축법회, 연등축제 등 각종 행사가 열린다. 부처님의 탄생 게송은 다음과 같다.

> 하늘 위와 하늘 아래에서 오직 내가 홀로 존귀하다.
> 온 세상이 모두 괴로움에 잠겨 있으니 내 마땅히 이를 편안하게 하리라.
>
> 《불본행집경(佛本行集經)》 권8

'출가재일'은 석가모니 부처님이 일체중생의 고통과 생사윤회의 해결을 위해 출가를 하신 날이다. 출가재일은 음력 2월 8일이다. 불자들은 이날 부처님을 본받아 '상구보리 하화중생'의 보살이 되겠다는 서원을 세우며 기념법회를 가진다.

> 내가 출가한 것은 병듦이 없고, 늙음이 없고, 죽음이 없고, 근심·걱정·번뇌가 없는 가장 안온하고 행복한 삶을 얻기 위해서였다.
>
> 《중아함경》 권56 라마경

Unit 1 **The Day the Buddha Came and Renunciation Day**

The four major Buddhist holidays are: Buddha's Birthday, Renunciation Day, Bodhi Day and Parinirvana Day. Buddha's Birthday, the birthday of Prince Siddhartha Gautama, is traditionally celebrated on the 8th day of the 4th lunar month. As the Buddha walked the bodhisattva path for countless lives and came to this world by his own choice, in Korea, his birthday is called "The Day the Buddha Came," although it is generally called Buddha's Birthday in the English-speaking world. The Day the Buddha Came is the biggest holiday among all the Buddhist holidays. As such, various celebratory events are held, including celebratory Dharma gatherings and the Lotus Lantern Festival. The Buddha recited the following verse at birth.

> Above the heavens and below the heavens I alone am most noble.
> All that exists in the three worlds is suffering, but I will bring comfort.
>
> -Vol. 8, *Sutra of the Collection of the Past Activities of the Buddha*

Renunciation Day is the day the Buddha left his palace to walk the spiritual path. The Buddha did so to save sentient beings from suffering and to resolve the great matter of samsara or the repeated cycle of birth and death. It is celebrated on the 8th day of the 2nd lunar month. On this day, Buddhists have commemorative Dharma gatherings to renew their vows to emulate the Buddha and become a bodhisattva who seeks enlightenment and teach others.

> I became a renunciant to earn a peaceful, happy life without sickness, old age, death, worries and delusions.
>
> -Vol. 56, *Madhyamagama* (MN 26)

Fill in the Blanks

1. The four _____ Buddhist holidays are: Buddha's Birthday, Renunciation Day, Bodhi Day and Parinirvana Day. (주요 또는 대)

2. Buddha's Birthday is the birthday of Prince _____ Gautama. (싯다르타)

3. It is traditionally celebrated on the 8th day of the ____ _____ _____. (음력 4월)

4. As the Buddha walked the _____ path for countless lives (보살)

5. The Buddha came to this world by his own _____. (선택 또는 의지)

6. In Korea, the Buddha's Birthday is called "The Day the Buddha _____." (오신)

7. It is the biggest holiday among all the Buddhist _____. (명절들)

8. As such, various _____ _____ are held. (축하 행사)

9. Above the heavens and below the heavens I alone am most _____. (고귀한)

10. Renunciation Day is the day the Buddha left his palace to walk the _____ _____.

    (수행길)

11. The Buddha did so to save _____ _____ from suffering. (중생)

12. On this day, Buddhists have _____ Dharma gatherings. (기념)

13. They renew their _____ to emulate the Buddha and become a bodhisattva. (서원)

Questions

1. What are the four major Buddhist holidays?

2. When is Buddha's Birthday celebrated?

3. How long did the Buddha walk the bodhisattva path?

4. What is Buddha's Birthday called in Korea?

5. When is Renunciation Day?

6. Do Buddhists renew their vows to emulate the Buddha on Renunciation Day?

성도재일, 열반재일

'성도재일'은 부처님께서 깨달음을 성취하신 날로, 음력 12월 8일이다. 불교에서 깨달음이란 석가모니 부처님만이 이룰 수 있는 신성한 영역이 아니라 누구나 수행정진을 통해 성취할 수 있는 것이다. 이날을 기념하여 선방의 수행자들은 일주일간 철야 용맹정진을 하며, 일반 사찰에서도 철야정진을 한다. 불자들은 부처님처럼 생사의 고해에서 벗어나 불국정토를 건설하겠다는 서원을 세우며 기념법회를 가진다.

> 많은 생을 윤회하면서 집 짓는 자를 찾아
> 나는 부질없이 치달려 왔다.
> 거듭되는 태어남은 괴로움이었다.
> 집 짓는 자여, 마침내 그대는 드러났구나.
> 그대 다시는 집을 짓지 못하리.
> 그대의 모든 골재들은 무너졌고
> 집의 서까래는 해체되었도다.
> 이제 마음은 업 형성을 멈추었고
> 갈애의 부서짐을 성취하였다.
>
> 부처님 오도송, 《법구경》 153-154

'열반재일'은 부처님께서 열반에 드신 날로 음력 2월 15일이다. 45년 동안 일체중생들의 고통을 치유해주시던 부처님이 80세로 반열반에 든 날이다. 이날 불자들 중에는 부처님께서 마지막 가르침을 내리시는 장면의 《열반경》을 함께 읽기도 한다. 또한 자신과 사랑하는 사람들의 죽음을 생각하고 무상의 진리를 다시 한 번 되새기기도 한다.

> 비구들이여, 참으로 그대들에게 당부하노니
> 형성된 것들은 소멸하기 마련인 법이다.
> 게으르지 말고 해야 할 바를 모두 성취하라.
>
> 《대반열반경》

Bodhi Day and Parinirvana Day

Bodhi Day, the 8th day of the 12th lunar month, is the day the Buddha attained enlightenment. In Buddhism, enlightenment is not reserved only for the Buddha as a sacred realm but is open to all who conduct dedicated practice. To mark this day nationwide, Seon halls conduct a seven-day non-stop practice without sleeping, and temples hold overnight Seon practice sessions. Buddhists have commemorative Dharma gatherings to renew their vows to be delivered from the suffering of birth and death and establish a Pure Land.

> Through the round of numerous births
> I roamed fruitlessly
> Seeking the house-builder
> Birth after birth was a suffering
> House-builder, you're uncovered at last
> You will not build a house again
> All your aggregates are collapsed
> All the rafters dismantled
> Now the mind has stopped the formation of karma,
> Attaining the end of craving
> > - Buddha's Verse of Enlightenment. 153-154, *Dhammapada*

Parinirvana Day, the 15th day of the 2nd lunar month, is the day the Buddha entered nirvana. The Buddha, who had healed the suffering of all sentient beings for 45 years, entered into complete nirvana at the age of 80 on this day. To mark this day, some Buddhists read together a part from the *Mahāparinirvāna Sūtra* (Pali: Mahāparinibbāna Sutta) which describes the Buddha's giving his last instructions. In addition they also remind themselves of their own and their loved ones' inevitable deaths, as well as of the truth of impermanence.

> Bhikkhus, I urge you to be always mindful:
> All composite things are impermanent
> Strive for your own liberation with vigilance
> > - *Mahāparinibbāna Sutta*

Fill in the Blanks

1. Bodhi Day is the day the Buddha _____ enlightenment. (얻다)

2. Enlightenment is not reserved only for the Buddha as a _____ _____. (성역)

3. To _____ this day nationwide. (기념하다)

4. _____ _____ conduct a seven-day non-stop practice without sleeping. (선방들)

5. Buddhists renew their vows to be _____ from the suffering of birth and death and establish a Pure Land. (벗어나다)

6. Parinirvana Day is the day the Buddha entered _____. (열반)

7. The Buddha _____ the suffering of all sentient beings for 45 years. (치유하다)

8. The Buddha entered into _____ _____ at the age of 80. (반열반)

9. They remind themselves of their own _____ deaths. (불가피한)

10. All _____ _____ are impermanent. (형성된 것)

11. Strive for your own liberation _____ _____. (방일하지 않게)

Questions

1. What is the day the Buddha attained enlightenment called?

2. Can only the Buddha attain enlightenment?

3. What do Seon halls do on Bodhi Day in Korea?

4. What is Parinirvana Day?

5. When is Parinirvana Day celebrated?

6. How old was the Buddha when he entered nirvana?

7. Which sutra describes the Buddha giving his last instructions?

1 천수경, 금강경

한국에서 법회를 할 때 가장 많이 독송하는 경전이 《천수경》이다. 《천수경》이란 '한량없는 손과 눈을 가지신 관세음보살의 넓고 크고 걸림 없는 대자비심을 간직한 큰 다라니'라는 뜻이다. 《천수경》은 많은 진언과 참회 그리고 서원으로 구성되어 있다. 특히 중생이 어떠한 어려움에 처했을 때 관세음보살님을 일념으로 부르면 모두 구제해준다는 대자비의 관음신앙이 천수경의 핵심이다. 아래는 천수경에 나오는 유명한 참회게이다.

> 죄는 본래 자성 없어 마음 따라 일어나니
> 마음 만약 없어지면 죄도 또한 사라지네
> 죄와 마음 사라져서 두 가지가 공적하면
> 이것을 곧 참다운 참회라고 이름하리

《금강경》은 대한불교조계종 소의경전으로서 한국 불자들이 가장 많이 듣고 배우는 경전 중 하나이다. '해공제일' 수보리와의 문답을 통해 공의 진리를 다양하고도 심오한 비유로 설법하고 있다. 공과 무상에 관한 많은 비유 중 가장 유명한 것이 바로 아래의 사구게이다.

> 일체의 형성되어진 것은
> 꿈과 같고 환상과 같고 물거품 같고 그림자 같으며
> 이슬과 같고 또한 번개와도 같으니
> 응당 이와 같이 관할지니라.

The Thousand Hands Sutra and the Diamond Sutra

The *Thousand Hands Sutra* is the most often recited sutra in Korean Dharma gatherings. The full title of the sutra translates literally as "great dharani which holds the vast, perfect and unhindered compassion of Avalokitesvara Bodhisattva who has innumerable hands and eyes." At its core, the sutra expresses faith in the Avalokitesvara of great compassion and teaches that if sentient beings in need call upon Avalokitesvara with single-minded concentration, they will be saved. Following is a noted excerpt from the *Thousand Hands Sutra*, the verse of repentance.

> Sins have no inherent self-nature but arise relying on mind
> When mind ceases, sins also cease
> When both sins and mind cease
> This is what is called true repentance

The *Diamond Sutra* is one of the main scriptures of the Jogye Order of Korean Buddhism. As such it is one of those sutras which Korean Buddhists most often listen to and learn. It explains the truth of emptiness through dialogues between the Buddha and Subhuti who has the special title "Foremost in Understanding the Doctrine of the Void." Of all the similes from the sutra used to describe emptiness and impermanence, the following is most well-known.

> All conditioned phenomena
> Are like dreams, illusions, bubbles, shadows,
> Dew and lightning
> Thus should you meditate upon them

1. The *Thousand Hands Sutra* is the most often _____ sutra in Korean Dharma gatherings. (독송되는)

2. _____ _____ which holds the vast, perfect and unhindered compassion of Avalokitesvara. (대다라니)

3. Avalokitesvara Bodhisattva who has _____ hands and eyes. (한량없는)

4. The sutra expresses faith in the Avalokitesvara of _____ _____. (대자비)

5. If sentient beings in need _____ _____ Avalokitesvara with single-minded concentration, they will be saved. (부르다)

6. The _____ of repentance. (게)

7. Sins have no inherent self-nature but arise _____ ___ mind. (연하여)

8. When mind _____, sins also cease. (멸하다)

9. The _____ _____ is one of the main scriptures of the Jogye Order of Korean Buddhism. (금강경)

10. It explains the truth of _____ through dialogues between the Buddha and Subhuti. (공성)

11. Of all the _____ from the sutra (비유들)

12. All conditioned phenomena are like dreams, illusions, _____. (물거품)

1. What is the most often recited sutra at Korean Dharma gatherings?

2. How many hands does Avalokitesvara Bodhisattva have?

3. According to the "verse of repentance," do sins have self-nature?

4. Is the *Diamond Sutra* an important sutra in the Jogye Order?

5. To whom does the Buddha keep asking questions in the *Diamond Sutra*?

6. What is the special title of Subhuti?

7. Does the *Diamond Sutra* often use similes?

② 반야심경, 아미타경

《반야심경》은 모든 대승경전 중에서도 가장 짧은 경전이지만 그 안에는 부처님이 말씀하신 모든 진리가 함축되어 들어 있다. 이 세상의 모든 것이 실체가 없는 공임을 철저하게 터득함으로써 지혜를 얻으면 결국 정각에 이른다고 설하고 있다. 현재 반야심경은 한글화되어 한국 불교의 모든 법회의식에서 독송된다.

> 사리자여! 모든 법은 공하여 나지도 멸하지도 않으며,
> 더럽지도 깨끗하지도 않으며, 늘지도 줄지도 않느니라.

《아미타경》은 극락세계에 대하여 설해놓은 경이다. 그래서 아미타불을 극락세계의 부처님이라 한다. 극락세계는 서쪽으로 10만 억 불토를 지나 있으며 그곳에 아미타부처님이 계시면서 항상 설법하고 있다고 한다. 거기에는 일체의 고통이 없으며, 자유롭고 안락하여 무한한 즐거움이 가득하므로 '극락'이라고 부른다고 밝히고 있다. 아미타불이 부처가 되기 전 전생의 이름이 법장 비구였다. 법장 비구는 중생구제의 48서원을 세우고 오랜 수행을 거듭한 끝에 아미타불이 되어 지금 극락세계에서 중생을 교화하고 한다. 아래는 그의 원력 중 하나이다.

> 제가 부처가 될 적에, 시방세계의 중생들이 저의 나라에 태어나고자 신심과 환희심을 내어 제 이름(아미타불)을 다만 열 번만 불러도 제 나라에 태어날 수 없다면, 저는 차라리 부처가 되지 않겠나이다.
>
> 법장 비구의 48원 중 '18원'

The Heart Sutra and the Amitabha Sutra

The *Heart Sutra* is the most concise sutra among all the Mahayana scriptures but contains all truths taught by the Buddha. It explains that awakening comes when one attains wisdom by thoroughly realizing that all phenomena are empty and without any real substance. The *Heart Sutra* has been translated into Hangeul (Korean script), and is recited in all Dharma gatherings in Korea.

Sāriputta! Alll dharmas are empty, non-arising, non-ceasing,
Non-defiled, non-pure, non-increasing and non-decreasing.

The *Amitabha Sutra* teaches about the Pure Land, or the Land of Ultimate Bliss. That's why Amitabha is called the Buddha of the Pure Land. It is located beyond hundreds of thousands of millions of buddhalands to the West. In this land, Amitabha resides and always teaches the Dharma. It is void of suffering and full of freedom, comfort and joy. Thus, it is called the "Ultimate Bliss." Before becoming a buddha, Amitabha was a monk named Dharmakāra in one of his previous lives. Dharmakāra made 48 vows to save sentient beings and practiced consistently for a long time. Eventually becoming a buddha, Amitabha is now edifying sentient beings in his Pure Land. Following is one of his vows.

If, when I attain buddhahood, sentient beings in the lands of the ten directions who desire to be born in my land, and sincerely and joyfully call my name (Amitabha) even ten times, are not reborn there, may I not attain perfect enlightenment.

-The 18th Vow from the *"Forty-Eight Vows of Dharmakāra"*

Fill in the Blanks

1. The *Heart Sutra* is the most _____ sutra among all the Mahayana scriptures. (간략한)

2. It explains that awakening comes when one _____ wisdom. (얻다)

3. All phenomena are empty and without any real _____. (실체)

4. The *Heart Sutra* has been _____ into Hangeul, or Korean script. (번역되다)

5. All dharmas are _____, non-arising, non-ceasing, (공한)

6. The *Amitabha Sutra* teaches about the _____ _____, or the Land of Ultimate Bliss. (정토)

7. In this land, Amitabha _____ and always teaches the Dharma. (거하다)

8. It is _____ of suffering and full of freedom, comfort and joy. (없는)

9. Amitabha was a monk named _____ in one of his previous lives. (법장)

10. Dharmakāra made 48 _____ to save sentient beings and practiced consistently for a long time. (원)

11. Sentient beings in the lands of the _____ _____. (시방)

Questions

1. What is the most concise sutra among all Mahayana scriptures?
2. Does the *Heart Sutra* say that all phenomena have substance?
3. Has the *Heart Sutra* been translated into Hangeul?
4. Are all dharmas non-defiled and non-pure?
5. Is Amitabha also called the Buddha of the Pure Land?
6. Is the Pure Land in the West?
7. Where does Amitabha reside?

사물

절에서 아침이나 저녁에 예불을 올릴 때면 먼저 사물의 소리를 공양한다. 사물은 법고, 범종, 목어, 운판을 일컬으며 주로 종각에 함께 배치한다.

법고는 땅에서 사는 축생을 제도하기 위해 치는데, 북소리가 널리 울려 퍼지듯 불법의 진리가 중생의 마음을 울려 깨우친다는 의미가 담겨 있다. 나무로 된 두 개의 북채로 마음 심(心) 자를 그리며 두드린다. 범종은 지옥에서 고통받는 중생들을 구제하기 위해 울린다. 또한 의식이나 행사 때 대중을 모이게 하거나 때를 알리기 위해 친다.

목어는 물에서 사는 어류를 제도하기 위한 것이다. 밤낮으로 눈을 뜨고 있는 물고기처럼 수행자도 그렇게 깨어 불법을 닦으라는 뜻이 담긴 법구이다. 운판은 날아다니는 조류를 제도하기 위한 것이다. 뭉게구름 형태의 법구로서 청동 혹은 철로 만든다. 목어와 운판은 아침저녁 예불의식 때에만 사용한다. 불교의식이 발달한 대승불교권에서만 볼 수 있는 법구들이다.

The Four Dharma Instruments

When the Dharma ceremony is conducted in the early mornings and evenings at temples, the sounds of the four Dharma instruments are offered first of all. The four Dharma instruments, found in most temple's Bell Pavilion, are: the Dharma drum, the temple bell, the wooden fish and the cloud-shaped gong.

The Dharma drum is sounded to save all land animals. The intent is to let the sound of the drum resonate in the minds of sentient beings and awaken them to the truth of the Buddha-Dharma just as the sound of the drum reverberates and spreads far and wide. The Dharma drum is sounded with two wooden sticks beating in the shape of the Chinese character "心" which means "mind." The temple bell is rung to save sentient beings suffering in Buddhist hell. It is also sounded to gather together sangha members for ceremonies and events and to mark special times or occasions.

The wooden fish is sounded to save waterborne creatures. It is a Dharma instrument which admonishes practitioners to be constantly awake to cultivate themselves just as fish keep their eyes open day and night. The cloud-shaped gong is sounded to save all winged creatures. It is made of bronze or iron. The wooden fish and cloud-shaped gong are sounded only at the morning and evening Dharma ceremonies. They can only be found in Mahayana Buddhist temples where Buddhist ceremonies and rituals are developed.

Fill in the Blanks

1. When the _____ _____ is conducted in the early mornings and evenings at temples. (예불)

2. The _____ _____ _____ , found in most temple's Bell Pavilion. (사물)

3. The _____ _____ is sounded to save all land animals. (법고)

4. The intent is to let the sound of the drum _____ in the minds of sentient beings. (울리다, 울려 퍼지다)

5. Just as the sound of the drum reverberates and spreads _____ and _____. (멀리)

6. The Dharma drum is _____ with two wooden sticks beating in the shape of the Chinese character "心" which means "mind." (울리다)

7. The temple bell is _____ to save sentient beings suffering in Buddhist hell. (울리다)

8. It is also sounded to _____ _____ sangha members for ceremonies and events. (불러 모으다)

9. The _____ _____ is sounded to save fish. (목어)

10. It is a Dharma instrument which _____ practitioners to be constantly awake. (경계하다, 타이르다)

11. Just as fish keep their eyes _____ day and night. (뜨고)

12. The cloud-shaped gong is sounded to save all _____ creatures. (날개 달린)

13. It is made of _____ or iron. (청동)

1. Are the sounds of the four instruments offered first at the morning and evening Dharma ceremonies at temples?

2. What is the building wherein you can find the four instruments?

3. Which of the four instruments is sounded to save all land animals?

4. Are the sticks with which the Dharma drum is beaten made of wood?

5. Which sentient beings does the temple bell intend to save?

6. Is the temple bell also rung to mark special occasions?

7. Is the wooden fish sounded to save waterborne creatures?

8. What is the cloud-shaped gong made of?

4 목탁, 죽비

불교의식에서 가장 널리 사용되는 불구인 목탁은 목어에서 유래되었다. 나무를 깎아 둥근 형태로 만들며 앞부분의 긴 입과 입 옆의 둥근 두 눈(구멍)으로 고기 형태를 나타내고 있다. 목탁은 수행자들이 잠을 자지 않는 물고기처럼 열심히 수행 정진할 것을 유도하는 도구이다. 조석예불이나 경전독송 할 때에 목탁을 사용하며 공양 시간이나 운력 시간을 알리는 신호로도 사용된다.

죽비는 좌선수행을 할 때 입선이나 방선을 알리거나 수행자의 졸음, 자세를 경책하기 위해서 사용한다. 또한 설법을 할 때나 공양할 때 그리고 절 수행을 할 때 사용한다. 입선·방선 시간을 알리는 작은 죽비와 졸음을 경책하기 위해 크게 만든 장군죽비가 있다. 죽비는 원래는 대나무로 만들었으나 요즘은 나무로도 많이 만든다.

Unit 4 The Moktak and the Seon Stick

The moktak, or wooden handbell, the most often used instrument in Buddhist ceremonies, evolved from the wooden fish. It is roundish in shape and carved from wood. The elongated opening in the front and the two round holes on both sides represent the mouth and eyes of a fish. As such, the moktak's purpose is to lead practitioners to practice fervently, just like the sleepless fish. The moktak is used to keep time in chanting or during the morning and evening Dharma ceremonies. It is also sounded to call monastics to meals or communal work.

The Jukbi, or Seon stick, comes in two sizes. The shorter Jukbi is used to announce the beginning and end of Seon meditation sessions while the longer one is used to prevent sleepiness during Seon meditation. They are also used during Dharma talks, meals and prostration practice. Seon sticks were originally made of bamboo, but recently, other kinds of wood are also used.

1. The moktak is the most _____ used instrument in Buddhist ceremonies. (자주)

2. Moktak is _____ in shape and carved from wood. (둥그스름한)

3. The _____ opening in the front represents the mouth of a fish. (긴)

4. The moktak's purpose is to lead practitioners to practice _____. (열심히)

5. The moktak is used to keep time in _____. (독송, 염불)

6. It is also sounded to call monastics to _____ or communal work. (공양)

7. The shorter Jukbi is used to _____ the beginning and end of Seon meditation sessions. (알리다)

8. The longer Jukbi is used to prevent _____ during Seon meditation. (졸음)

9. They are also used during Dharma talks, meals and _____ _____. (절수행)

10. _____ _____ were originally made of bamboo. (죽비)

1. Is the moktak the most often used instrument in Buddhist ceremonies?

2. Did the wooden handbell evolve from the wooden fish?

3. What do the two round holes on both sides of the moktak represent?

4. What is the moktak's purpose?

5. Is the moktak used to call monastics to communal work?

6. Does the Seon stick come in one size?

7. Is the Seon stick an indispensable instrument in Seon halls?

8. Is the Seon stick only used for Seon meditation?

9. What were the Seon sticks originally made of?

5 가사, 장삼

가사(袈裟)는 수행승들이 입는 법의로 산스크리트어 캬사야(kāṣāya)를 소리나는 대로 옮긴 말이다. 가사는 속세 사람들이 버린 헌 천을 조각조각 꿰매어 만들어 입었다는 의미에서 납의(衲衣), 죽은 시체를 감싸던 천으로 만들었다고 해서 분소의(糞掃衣), 보시와 공덕을 짓게 한다는 의미에서 복전의(福田衣)라 부른다. 이 같은 이유로 가사는 청정과 무소유의 대명사가 됐으며 선종에서는 발우와 함께 스승과 제자 사이에 법을 잇는 증표로서 사용되고 있다.

장삼은 스님들이 가사 속에 받쳐 입는 소매의 품이 큰 옷이다. 원래 더운 지방인 인도에서는 착용하지 않았으나 불교가 중국으로 전해지면서 의생활 풍습과 기후 등이 다른 까닭에 장삼을 입고 가사를 입는 것이 정착되었다. 우리나라에서는 가사와 장삼을 일상생활에서는 입지 않으며 예불이나 법공양 등의 의식 때만 입는다.

Monastic Robes: Gasa and Jangsam

Ceremonial monastic robes called "gasa," a transliteration of the Sanskrit word "kāṣāya," are Dharma garments worn by Buddhist monastic practitioners. They are also called "patchwork robes" because they used to be made by patching together cloth scraps thrown away by others. They are also called "robes made of rubbish-heap rags" as they used to be made from shrouds, or "robes of the field of merit" as they help the donor to cultivate generosity and gain merit. For these reasons, gasa began to symbolize purity and non-possession. In Seon Schools, gasa, along with alms bowls, are used by teachers and disciples to designate a Dharma heir.

The long robes called jangsam have very wide sleeves. Monastics wear jangsam under their gasa (kāṣāya). It is not worn in the semi-tropical regions of India. As Buddhism was introduced to China, due to different dressing habits and the colder climate, wearing jangsam became the norm. In Korea, gasa and jangsam are not worn in daily life but worn only on formal occasions like Dharma ceremonies and Dharma offerings.

Fill in the Blanks

1. Ceremonial monastic robes are called "gasa," a _____ of the Sanskrit word "kāṣāya." (소리나는 대로 옮긴 번역)

2. Gasa are _____ _____ worn by Buddhist monastic practitioners. (법의)

3. They are also called "_____ robes" because they used to be made by patching together cloth scraps thrown away by others. (납의)

4. They are also called "robes made of _____ _____" as they used to be made from shrouds. (분소의)

5. They are also called "robes of the _____ of a_____" as they help the donor to cultivate generosity and gain merit. (복전의)

6. For these reasons, gasa began to symbolize _____ and non-possession. (청정)

7. In Seon Schools, gasa, along with alms bowls, are used by teachers and disciples to designate a _____ _____. (법을 이은 사람)

8. The long robes called jangsam have very _____ _____. (넓은 소매)

9. Monastics wear jangsam _____ their gasa (kāṣāya). (아래에)

10. As Buddhism was _____ to China, wearing jangsam became the norm. (도입되다)

11. In Korea, gasa and jangsam are not worn in _____ _____. (일상생활)

1. Is "gasa" a transliteration of the Sanskrit word "kāṣāya?"
2. Are ceremonial monastic robes also called patchwork robes?
3. Why are ceremonial monastic robes called "robes of the field of merit?"
4. Which virtues do gasa symbolize?
5. What do Seon masters give to a disciple to designate them as a Dharma heir?
6. Do monastics wear jangsam over their gasa?
7. Is Jangsam worn in India or Southeast Asia?
8. Why did Chinese and Korean monastics begin to wear jangsam?
9. Do Korean monks and nuns wear gasa in daily life?

1 일주문, 불이문

일주문은 '산문'이라고도 하는데, 산사에 들어서면 맨 먼저 만나게 되는 문이다. 기둥이 일직선상으로 한 줄로 서 있다는 데에서 일주문이란 이름이 유래하였다. 사찰에 들어서면서 세속의 번뇌를 떨쳐내고 마음을 하나로 모아 진리의 세계로 들어가는 것을 상징한다. 이 문을 경계로 문 밖을 속계(俗界)라 하고 문 안을 진계(眞界)라 하니, 일주문은 사바세계에서 정토세계로, 이 언덕에서 저 언덕으로 가는 첫째 관문인 것이다.

불이문(不二門)은 부처님 계신 법당으로 가는 마지막 문이다. 불이(不二)의 진리로써 모든 번뇌를 씻어 버리고 해탈을 이루어 부처가 된다고 하여 해탈문이라고도 부른다. 불이는 둘이 아닌 경지로, 하나를 말하거나 같음을 의미하는 것도 아니다. 너와 나, 생과 사, 번뇌와 보리 등 모든 상대적인 것이 둘이 아닌 비이원성을 의미한다.

> "어떻게 하는 것이 보살의 불이법문에 들어가는 방법인가"에 대해, 유마 거사는 침묵으로 대답을 대신하였다. 이에 대해 문수보살은 "장하고 장하다! 여기(유마의 침묵)는 문자도 언어도 없으니, 참으로 불이법문에 들어가는 것이다"
>
> 《유마경》

Unit 1 **The One Pillar Gate and the Gate of Non-Duality**

The One Pillar Gate, which is called "Iljumun"or "Sanmun" in Korean, is the first gate to encounter when visiting mountain temples. The One Pillar Gate is named after the fact that its pillars are lined up in one straight line. It symbolizes entering the temple with a oneness of mind toward the world of truth while putting aside worldly desires. It is considered a boundary between the secular and the Dharma world, and is the first gateway which crosses from "this shore" to the "other shore."

The Gate of Non-Duality (Kor. Burimun) is the last gate to pass before approaching the Dharma hall where the Buddha resides. It is also called the Liberation Gate as one can attain liberation after washing away all afflictions with the truth of non-duality. Non-duality refers to the state of "not being two," which means acknowledging neither identification nor differentiation, but rather embracing non-dualism in which the relative aspects of things such as you and I, birth and death, and afflictions and enlightenment are not two.

> "What is the way for bodhisattvas to enter the Dharma gate of non-duality?" The layman Vimalakirti answered the question by remaining silent. Then, Manjusri Bodhisattva said, "Well done! Well done! There is neither letters nor words in this (Vimalakirti's silence), which is the way to enter the Dharma gate of non-duality."
>
> *- Vimalakirti Sutra*

Fill in the Blanks

1. The One _____ Gate, which is called "Iljumun" or "Sanmun" in Korean, (기둥)

2. Iljumun is the first gate to encounter when visiting _____ _____. (산사)

3. The One Pillar Gate is named after the fact that its pillars are lined up in

    _____ _____ _____. (한 줄로)

4. It symbolizes entering the temple with a _____ of mind toward the world of truth. (하나)

5. It is considered a _____ between the secular and the Dharma world. (경계)

6. It is the first gateway which crosses from "this shore" to the "_____ _____." (저 언덕)

7. The Gate of _____ (Kor. Burimun) is the last gate to pass before approaching the Dharma hall. (불이문)

8. It is also called the _____ Gate as one can attain liberation after washing away all afflictions with the truth of non-duality. (해탈문)

9. Non-duality refers to the state of "not being _____." (둘)

10. In non-dualism the _____ aspects of things such as you and I and birth and death are not two. (상대적)

11. What is the _____ for bodhisattvas to enter the Dharma gate of non-duality?" (방법)

12. The layman _____ answered the question by remaining silent. (유마)

1. What is the first gate one encounters when visiting mountain temples?

2. What does the straight alignment of the pillars of the One Pillar Gate symbolize?

3. The One Pillar Gate is considered a boundary between what two worlds?

4. What is the other name of the Gate of Non-Duality?

5. In the world of non-duality, are birth and death considered two separate things?

6. How did Vimalakirti answer the question posed by Manjusri?

7. Did Manjusri consider silence as the way to enter the Dharma gate of non-duality?

2 금강문, 천왕문

금강문은 불법의 수호신인 금강역사를 모시는 문으로 일주문과 천왕문 사이에 세워진다. 금강역사는 불탑 또는 사찰의 문 양쪽을 지키는 수문신장의 역할을 담당하며 인왕역사라고도 한다. 우리나라 사찰에서는 일반적으로 천왕문의 대문에다 금강역사의 모습을 그려 놓은 경우가 많고 때로는 천왕문 안에 금강역사 조각상을 세우기도 한다. 그러나 금강역사만을 별도로 모신 금강문을 천왕문 앞쪽에 세우는 경우도 종종 볼 수 있다.

천왕문은 불법을 수호하는 사천왕을 모신 건물이다. 사천왕은 동서남북의 네 방향을 지키므로 '사천왕'이라 부른다. 사천왕의 구분은 어떤 방위에 있는가와 손에 지니고 있는 것에 의해진다. 동방의 지국천왕은 비파를, 남방의 증장천왕은 보검을, 서방의 광목천왕은 용과 여의주를, 북방의 다문천왕은 보탑을 가지고 있다. 그리고 사천왕은 악귀를 밟고 있는데 천하의 악에 대한 제압을 상징하는 것이다. 이것과 아울러 사천왕은 해당 사찰을 수호하고 불법을 보호하는 역할을 한다.

Unit 2 The Diamond Gate and the Gate of Heavenly Kings

Standing between the One Pillar Gate and the Gate of Heavenly Kings, the Diamond Gate enshrines Vajrapanis, protectors of the Buddha-Dharma. In Korean, a Vajrapani is called either "Geumgang-nyeoksa" or "Inwang-nyeoksa." The Vajrapanis serve as guardians of a pagoda or a temple gate. In Korean temples, Vajrapanis are generally painted on the Gate of Heavenly Kings, but sometimes statues of them are enshrined inside the gate. However, in some cases, a Diamond Gate is established wherein Vajrapanis are exclusively enshrined.

The Gate of Heavenly Kings is dedicated to the four heavenly kings in charge of protecting the Buddha-Dharma. They are called "four heavenly kings" as they guard the four cardinal directions of north, east, south and west. They can be distinguished by which direction they guard and what they hold in their hands. In the east, Dhṛtarāṣṭra (He who maintains the state) stands holding a lute (pipa). In the south, Virūḍhaka (He who enlarges) stands holding a sword. In the west, Virūpākṣa (He who sees all) stands holding a dragon and a wish-fulfilling jewel (cintamani). In the north, Vaiśravaṇa (He who hears everything) stands holding a stupa. All the four heavenly kings trample demons underfoot, symbolizing their control over all evil spirits in the universe. In addition, they have the role of guarding the temple and protecting the Buddha-Dharma.

Fill in the Blanks

1. The Diamond Gate enshrines _____, protectors of the Buddha-Dharma. (금강역사)

2. The Vajrapanis serve as _____ of a pagoda or a temple gate. (수호자)

3. In Korean temples, Vajrapanis are generally _____ on the Gate of Heavenly Kings. (그려지다)

4. Sometimes statues of them are _____ inside the gate. (모시다)

5. The Gate of Heavenly Kings is dedicated to the four heavenly kings in _____ of protecting the Buddha-Dharma. (담당)

6. They are called "four heavenly kings" as they guard the four _____ _____ of north, east, south and west. (기본 방위)

7. They can be distinguished by which direction they guard and what they _____ in their hands. (들다)

8. In the east, Dhṛtarāṣṭra (He who maintains the _____) stands holding a _____. (나라, 비파)

9. In the south, Virūḍhaka (He who enlarges) stands holding a _____. (검)

10. In the west, Virūpākṣa (He who sees all) stands holding a dragon and _____. (여의주)

11. In the north, Vaiśravaṇa (He who hears everything) stands holding a _____. (탑)

12. All the four heavenly kings _____ demons underfoot. (밟다)

13. In addition, they have the role of guarding the temple and protecting the _____. (불법)

Questions

1. Which gate stands between the One Pillar Gate and the Gate of Heavenly Kings in some Korean temples?

2. Who are the Vajrapanis?

3. To whom is the Gate of Heavenly Kings dedicated?

4. Which direction does the heavenly king named "He who maintains the state" guard?

5. What do the heavenly kings trample under foot?

3 불화

불교를 소재로 하여 그린 그림을 불화(佛畵)라고 한다. 불화는 부처님의 수행 모습과 교화하시는 모습을 시각화하여 불교를 쉽게 이해시키고 신심을 우러나게 하는 데 있다. 불화는 부처님 전생의 이야기인 본생도, 부처님의 일대기인 팔상도, 마음을 찾는 것을 소를 찾는 것에 비유한 심우도, 불법을 보호하는 신중탱화 등이 있다. 여기에서 탱화(幀畵)는 벽에 거는 그림이며, 벽화는 벽에 직접 그린 그림이다. 괘불은 야외에서 의식을 거행할 때 내다 거는 높이 3~10미터 정도의 거대한 불화이다.

Unit 3 Buddhist Painting

"Buddhist painting" refers to any painting which has Buddhism as its subject matter. The main purpose of Buddhist paintings is to help people understand Buddhism and have deeper faith in Buddhism by visualizing a buddha engaged in Buddhist practice or Dharma talks. Some outstanding Buddhist paintings are: "Bonsaengdo" which depicts Jataka stories about the previous lives of the Buddha; "Palsangdo" which depicts the eight main events of the Buddha's life; "Simudo" or Ten Ox-Herding pictures, which describe "searching for an ox" as a metaphor for "looking into one's true nature"; and "Sinjung Taenghwa" which depicts protective deities who protect the Buddha-Dharma. Buddhist painting can be broadly divided into three types. First, "taenghwa," a Korean transliteration of "thanka," is a scrolled painting hung on the wall. Second, a wall painting or mural is painted directly on the wall. Third, "gwaebul" is a large scroll painting, approximately 3-10 meters high, used for special outdoor ceremonies.

1. "Buddhist painting" refers to any painting which has Buddhism as its _____ _____. (주제)

2. The main _____ of Buddhist paintings is to help people understand Buddhism. (목적)

3. To help people have deeper faith in Buddhism by _____ a buddha engaged in Buddhist practice or Dharma talks. (눈앞에 그리다)

4. "Bonsaengdo" which depicts Jataka stories about the _____ _____ of the Buddha; (전생)

5. "Palsangdo" which _____ the eight main events of the Buddha's life; (그리다)

6. Ten Ox-Herding pictures, which describe "searching for an ox" as a _____ for "looking into one's true nature"; (비유, 은유)

7. "Sinjung Taenghwa" which depicts protective _____ who protect the Buddha-Dharma. (신격)

8. Buddhist painting can be _____ divided into three types. (넓게)

9. First, "taenghwa" is a _____ painting hung on the wall. (두루말이의)

10. Second, a wall painting or mural is painted _____ on the wall. (직접)

11. Third, "gwaebul" is used for special _____ _____. (야외의식)

Questions

1. What do Buddhist paintings have as their subject matter?

2. Is helping people have deeper faith in Buddhism one of the purposes of Buddhist paintings?

3. What do Bonsaengdo paintings depict?

4. Do oxen or bulls appear in the Ten Ox-Herding pictures?

5. Is taenghwa a kind of mural?

6. What kind of Buddhist paintings are used instead of buddha statues for outdoor ceremonies?

탑, 승탑

탑은 본래 부처님의 사리나 유품을 봉안하기 위해 만든 조형 건축물이다. 산스크리트어 'Stupa'는 부처님의 묘탑(墓塔)을 의미한다. 《대반열반경》에 전하는 바에 의하면 부처님이 입멸하신 뒤 여덟 나라 국왕이 부처님 사리를 8등분하여 각기 탑을 세우고 봉안했다는 기록이 있다. 하지만 후세에 이르러 묘탑으로서의 성격은 흐려지고 가람을 장엄하는 요소로 자리하게 되면서 동아시아에서는 점차로 'stupa'보다는 'pagoda'라고 불리게 되었다. 탑 안에 들어가는 내용도 부처님의 사리 이외에 불상, 경전류 등이 모셔지게 되었다. 탑에 대한 예배는 먼저 탑을 향해 합장 반배를 한 다음 합장한 채 오른쪽으로 세 번 혹은 그 이상 돌고 나서 다시 합장 반배하여 끝낸다.

불탑이 부처님의 사리를 봉안한 묘탑이었다면 승탑은 고승의 사리나 유골을 안치한 묘탑이다. 불탑이 사찰의 중심부에 있다면 승탑은 변두리나 경내 밖에 따로 조성한다. 승탑에는 거기 따르는 탑비(塔碑)가 건립되어 주인공의 행적이나 그 시대의 역사를 알 수 있는 귀중한 자료가 되기도 한다.

Stupas and Seungtaps (Monks' Stupa)

A stupa is a structure constructed originally to enshrine the Buddha's relics or keepsakes. In Sanskrit, "stupa" means the Buddha's grave. According to the *Mahaparinirvana Sutra*, after the Buddha's nirvana, the kings of eight countries divided the Buddha's relics among themselves and each of them built a stupa to enshrine them. However, as time went by, stupas gradually lost their original function and instead became magnificent adornment of the temple. In East Asia, they gradually came to be called "pagodas" rather than "stupas." The contents enshrined inside also began to include statues of the Buddha and sutras instead of his relics. When venerating a stupa or pagoda, one should offer a half-bow with palms together, circumambulate it three times or more clockwise while maintaining joined palms, and then offer a half-bow again.

A stupa is a grave which enshrines the Buddha's relics, but a "seungtap" (monks' stupa) is a grave which enshrines the relics or remains of an eminent monk. A stupa is situated in the center of a temple compound, but a seungtap is placed on the outskirts of a temple. A seungtap is usually accompanied by a monument listing the great monk's deeds, making them a valuable resource on the history of the era.

Fill in the Blanks

1. A stupa is a structure constructed originally to enshrine the Buddha's _____ or

   keepsakes. (사리)

2. In Sanskrit, "stupa" means the Buddha's _____. (묘)

3. According to the Parinirvana Sutra, after the Buddha's _____, the kings of eight

   countries divided the Buddha's relics among themselves. (열반)

4. Each of the eight countries built a stupa to _____ the relics. (모시다)

5. Stupas gradually lost their original function and instead became magnificent

   _____ of the temple. (장엄)

6. The _____ enshrined inside also began to include statues of the Buddha and sutras

   instead of his relics. (내용물)

7. When venerating a stupa or pagoda, one should offer a _____ with palms together,

   _____ it three times or more clockwise. (반배, 돌다)

8. A "seungtap" (monks' stupa) is a grave which enshrines the relics or remains of an

   _____ _____. (고승)

9. A stupa is situated in the center of a temple _____, but a seungtap is placed on

   the _____ of a temple. (경내, 외곽)

1. What was a stupa originally constructed to enshrine?
2. How many kings divided the Buddha's relics after his nirvana?
3. What did the eight countries build to enshrine the Buddha's relics?
4. These days in East Asia, what is usually enshrined inside a pagoda?
5. What is a seungtap?
6. Do all monks have their own seungtap after they pass away?
7. What is engraved on a monument which accompanies a seungtap?

석등은 야외에서 불을 밝히기 위해 만들어진 석조물이다. 그것은 부처님이 설법하실 때 도량에 등을 밝혀놓고 한 데서 유래한다. 후대에 석등이 발달하면서 가람 배치상의 건조물이 되었다. 옛날에는 법당이나 불탑 앞에 외등을 설치했는데, 근래에는 좌우대칭으로 두 개의 석등을 세우는 경우가 많다. 석등은 마음을 밝히고, 세상의 어둠을 일깨우며, 피안의 세계로 인도하는 지혜의 등불이다.

풍경은 법당이나 탑의 처마에 작은 종과 종 안에 물고기 모양의 금속판을 매달아 소리를 나게 하는 것이다. 바람이 불 때마다 은은하게 울리는 풍경소리는 절의 운치를 더해줄 뿐 아니라 주변 사람들의 마음을 어루만져준다. 하지만 풍경의 역할은 수행자의 방일이나 나태함을 깨우치기 위한 것이다. 물고기 모양의 얇은 금속판이 달린 이유는 물고기가 잠을 잘 때도 눈을 감지 않는 것처럼 수행자는 잠을 줄이고 언제나 깨어 있어야 한다는 뜻이다.

Stone Lanterns and Wind Bells

A stone lantern is a lantern carved from stone to lighten the darkness outside. It originated with the Buddha who lit up the monastery when giving Dharma talks. As time passed, the stone lantern became a regular fixture in every Buddhist temple. In the past, a single lantern was placed either in front of the Dharma hall or a pagoda. However, lately, pairs of stone lanterns are frequently used for symmetry. The stone lantern represents the light of wisdom which brightens up the mind, awakens the world from darkness and leads people to nirvana.

Wind bells are hung on the eaves of Dharma halls or pagodas. A fish-shaped metal piece hangs from the bell's clapper, causing it to strike the bell when the wind blows. The gentle ring of the bell in the breeze not only adds classical beauty to the temple but also soothes the hearts of anyone nearby. The main function of the wind bell is, however, to arouse practitioners from sloth and torpor. The metal fish reminds practitioners to be always awake, just as fish keep their eyes open even during sleep.

1. A stone lantern is a lantern carved from stone to _____ the darkness outside. (밝히다)

2. It originated with the Buddha who _____ _____ the monastery when giving Dharma talks. (등을 켜다)

3. As time _____, the stone lantern became a regular fixture in every Buddhist temple. (시간이 흐르다)

4. In the past, a _____ lantern was placed either in front of the Dharma hall or a pagoda. (단일)

5. However, lately, pairs of stone lanterns are frequently used for _____. (대칭)

6. The stone lantern represents the light of _____ which brightens up the mind. (지혜)

7. Wind bells are hung on the _____ of Dharma halls or pagodas. (처마)

8. A fish-shaped metal piece hangs from the bell's _____, causing it to strike the bell when the wind blows. (추)

9. The gentle ring of the bell in the breeze _____ the hearts of anyone nearby. (어루만져주다)

10. The main function of the wind bell is, however, to arouse practitioners from _____ and _____. (나태, 방일)

1. Where does the stone lantern originate from?
2. How many stone lanterns were placed in front of the Dharma hall in the past?
3. What does the stone lantern represent?
4. Where are wind bells hung?
5. What does the metal piece hanging from the wind bell look like?
6. What is the main function of the wind bell?
7. Is the ring of the wind bell loud or soft?

해인사의 팔만대장경과 장경판전

팔만대장경은 고려시대인 1251년에 완성된 목판대장경이다. 750여 년이 지난 지금도 거의 완벽한 목판본으로 남아 있는 해인사 팔만대장경은 현존하는 목판대장경 중 가장 오래된 것이다. 대장경은 부처님의 가르침을 담은 경장, 지켜야 할 계율을 담은 율장, 경장에 대한 해설과 주석을 담은 논장으로 구성되어 있다. 고려시대 인쇄술의 발전을 보여주는 팔만대장경의 81,258판은 불서의 간행을 용이하게 하여 불교의 연구와 확산을 도왔다. 2007년에 팔만대장경의 경판이 세계기록유산에 등재되었다.

유네스코에서는 1995년 팔만대장경의 경판을 봉안한 해인사 장경판전을 세계문화유산으로 지정하였다. 이는 기계문명을 사용하지 않고도 목판을 700여 년 동안 잘 보존한 장경판전 건물의 과학적 설계를 인정한 것이었다. 장경판전은 경판을 보호하고 오랫동안 보존할 수 있게 하는 기능을 가지고 있고, 최적의 환기와 온도로 경판의 변형과 부식을 방지하도록 설계하였다.

Unit 1 **The Tripitaka Koreana and the Janggyeong Panjeon at Haein-sa Temple**

The Tripitaka Koreana or "Palman Daejanggyeong" are printing woodblocks produced in 1251 during the Goryeo Dynasty. Preserved in almost perfect condition, the Tripitaka Koreana enshrined at Haein-sa Temple is the oldest extant woodblock tripitaka in the world. A tripitaka contains the entire Buddhist canon divided into three categories, or "baskets": the sutra basket contains the Buddha's teachings; the vinaya basket contains the precepts and rules to be observed by Buddhist monks and nuns; and the Abhidharma basket contains annotations and commentaries on the sutras. These 81,258 woodblocks epitomize the development of Goryeo era printing technology. These woodblocks facilitated the publication of Buddhist books, thereby furthering research into and the dissemination of Buddhism. In 2007, the printing woodblocks of the Tripitaka Koreana were registered in the UNESCO Memory of the World as a documentary heritage.

UNESCO also designated Haein-sa's Janggyeong Panjeon, the repository of the Tripitaka Koreana woodblocks, as a World Cultural Heritage in 1995. This was in recognition of the Janggyeong Panjeon's scientific design which has successfully preserved the woodblocks for more than 700 years without relying on modern technology. The Janggyeong Panjeon has built-in design features which can protect and preserve the printing woodblocks for extended periods. Designed to maintain optimum temperature and air circulation, the Janggyeong Panjeon prevents deformation and decay of the woodblocks.

Fill in the Blanks

1. The _____ _____, or "Palman Daejanggyeong," are printing woodblocks produced in 1251. (팔만대장경)

2. The Tripitaka Koreana enshrined at Haein-sa Temple is the oldest _____ woodblock tripitaka in the world. (현존하는)

3. A tripitaka contains the entire Buddhist canon divided into three categories, or "_____." (바구니)

4. The sutra basket contains the Buddha's _____. (가르침)

5. The vinaya basket contains the _____ and rules to be observed by Buddhist monks and nuns. (계율)

6. The Abhidharma basket contains _____ and commentaries on the sutras. (주석)

7. These 81,258 _____ epitomize the development of Goryeo era printing technology. (목판)

8. These woodblocks _____ the publication of Buddhist books. (촉진하다)

9. In 2007, the printing woodblocks of the Tripitaka Koreana were registered in the UNESCO Memory of the World as a _____ _____. (기록유산)

10. UNESCO also _____ Haein-sa's Janggyeong Panjeon as a World Cultural Heritage in 1995. (지정하다)

11. Janggyeong Panjeon has successfully _____ the woodblocks for more than 700 years. (보존하다)

12. It is designed to maintain _____ temperature and air circulation. (적정의)

13. The Janggyeong Panjeon prevents _____ and decay of the woodblocks. (변형)

Questions

1. When were the woodblocks of the Tripitaka Koreana produced?

2. Are the woodblocks of the Tripitaka Koreana preserved in good condition?

3. What is the oldest extant woodblock tripitaka in the world?

4. What does "tripitaka" mean in plain English?

5. Which basket holds the collected teachings of the Buddha?

6. How many printing woodblocks does the Tripitaka Koreana have?

7. When was the Tripitaka Koreana registered as a Memory of the World?

8. Does the Janggyeong Panjeon utilize modern technology?

9. Does the Janggyeong Panjeon maintain optimum temperature?

경주의 불국사와 석굴암

경주 토함산 서쪽에 위치한 불국사는, 신라인이 그린 부처님의 나라 곧 이상적인 피안의 세계를 지상에 옮겨 놓은 사찰이다. 즉《법화경》에 근거한 석가모니불의 사바세계와《무량수경》에 근거한 아미타불의 극락세계 및《화엄경》에 근거한 비로자나불의 연화장세계를 형상화한 것이다. 이처럼 불교교리가 사찰 건축물을 통해 잘 형상화된 예는 아시아에서도 그 유례를 찾기 어렵다. 또한 사찰의 건축구조와 그 내부의 조형물들, 즉 석가탑과 다보탑, 청운교와 백운교, 연화교와 칠보교 등은 세계적으로 우수성을 인정받는 기념비적인 예술품이다. 게다가 불국사에서는 지금도 승가대학과 선원에서 수많은 스님들이 경전 공부와 참선 수행을 하고 있어 살아 있는 한국불교의 전통을 생생히 볼 수 있는 곳이기도 하다.

경주 토함산 정상에 못 미친 깊숙한 곳에서 동해를 향해 앉아 있는 석굴암은 완벽하고 빼어난 조각과 독창적 건축으로 전 세계에 이름이 높다. 8세기 중엽 통일신라 문화의 황금기에 건립된 석굴암은 불교사상과 함께 매우 발달한 수리적 원리를 바탕으로 한 고도의 건축 기술, 뛰어난 조형감각으로 완성되었다. 석굴암에서 느끼는 장엄미와 숭고미는 이러한 바탕과 그 속에 내재하는 조화율에 있는 것이다.

석굴암은 인도나 중국의 천연석굴과는 달리 인공석굴이다. 백색의 화강암재를 사용하여 토함산 중턱에 인공으로 석굴을 축조하였다. 그 내부 공간에는 본존불인 석가여래불상을 중심으로 그 주벽에 보살상 및 제자상과 금강역사상, 천왕상 등 총 39체의 불상이 조각되어 있다. 특히 석굴암의 본존불이 계신 곳에서 보는 장엄한 일출은 예로부터 유명하다.

이처럼 경주는 찬란한 불교문명을 꽃피웠던 신라시대의 문화가 고스란히 남아 있기에 도시 전체가 일종의 박물관이다. 이런 연유로 2000년에는 경주시가 유네스코 세계유산목록에 등재되었다. 이에 앞서, 신라불교미술의 걸작으로 손꼽히는 불국사와 석굴암은 1995년에 이미 유네스코 세계유산에 등재되었다.

Gyeongju's Bulguk-sa Temple and Seokguram Grotto

Bulguk-sa, or Buddhaland Temple, is located west of Toham-san Mountain in Gyeongju. Bulguk-sa is the recreation on earth of the world of the Buddha as envisioned by the Silla people, that is, the ideal world of the "other shore." In other words, Silla artisans created the secular world of Sakyamuni Buddha based on the *Lotus Sutra*; the Pure Land of Amitabha Buddha mentioned in the *Sutra of Immeasurable Life*; and the Lotus-Treasury World of Vairocana Buddha mentioned in the *Flower Adornment Sutra*. This excellent embodiment of the Buddhist tenets in temple architecture is unparalleled even in Asia. In addition, the design of Bulguk-sa and the structures within it such as Seokga-tap and Dabo-tap pagodas, as well as Cheongun-gyo, Baegun-gyo, Yeonhwa-gyo and Chilbo-gyo bridges, are all world-renowned monumental artworks. Even today, a number of monks study scriptures and practice Seon meditation in Bulguk-sa's Monastic College and Seon Hall. Bulguk-sa truly represents the living traditions of Korean Buddhism.

Seokguram Grotto is situated on Toham-san Mountain, just below the summit, facing the East Sea. It has earned worldwide acclaim for its exquisite sculpture and creative architecture. Established in the mid-8th century during the golden era of the United Silla Dynasty, Seokguram was built using highly developed architectural skills and superb craftsmanship based on Buddhist thought and advanced mathematical principles. The magnificent and sublime beauty Seokguram emanates originates from these principles and the grotto's innate balance of harmony.

Unlike the natural grottos of India and China, Seokguram is a manmade grotto. White granite was used to create a grotto on the upper slope of Toham-san Mountain. Inside the grotto, Sakyamuni is enshrined as the main Buddha, and on the surrounding walls, there are 39 engravings of bodhisattvas, disciples, Vajrapanis and heavenly guardians. A view of the sunrise over the sea, which is visible from near the seated Sakyamuni Buddha's perch, is renowned for its magnificence.

As Gyeongju has preserved intact the culture of the Silla era which nurtured a glorious Buddhist civilization, the whole city is a living museum. As such, UNESCO designated certain parts of Gyeongju as Gyeongju Historic Areas and listed them in its World Cultural Heritage list in 2000. Prior to this, UNESCO also designated Bulguk-sa Temple and Seokguram Grotto, masterpieces of Silla Buddhist art, as World Cultural Heritage sites in 1995.

Fill in the Blanks

1. Bulguk-sa is located _____ of Toham-san Mountain in Gyeongju. (서쪽에)

2. Bulguk-sa is the recreation on earth of the world of the Buddha as _____ by the Silla people. (상상하다, 그리다)

3. Silla artisans created the secular world of Sakyamuni Buddha _____ on the Lotus Sutra. (근거한)

4. The _____ _____ of Amitabha Buddha mentioned in the Sutra of Immeasurable Life. (극락세계, 정토)

5. This excellent embodiment of the Buddhist tenets in temple architecture is _____ even in Asia. In addition. (유례가 없다)

6. They are all _____ monumental artworks. (세계적인)

7. Bulguk-sa truly represents the _____ traditions of Korean Buddhism. (살아 있는)

8. Unlike the natural grottos of India and China, Seokguram is a _____ _____. (인공석굴)

9. A view of the sunrise over the sea, which is visible from near the seated Sakyamuni Buddha's perch, is renowned for its _____. (장엄)

10. Seokguram Grotto is situated on Toham-san Mountain, just below the _____. (정상)

11. It has earned worldwide acclaim for its exquisite _____ and creative architecture. (조각)

12. Established in the mid-8th century during the _____ _____ of the United Silla Dynasty, (황금기)

13. As Gyeongju has preserved intact the culture of the Silla era, the whole city is a living _____. (박물관)

14. As such, UNESCO designated certain parts of Gyeongju as Gyeongju _____ Areas and listed them in its World Cultural Heritage list. (역사적인)

Questions

1. Where is Bulguk-sa located in Gyeongju?

2. Did the Silla people recreate the ideal world at Bulguk-sa Temple?

3. Does the architecture of Bulguk-sa embody the Buddhist tenets?

4. Does Bulguk-sa have many world-renowned artworks?

5. Is Seokguram a natural grotto?

6. Were mathematical principles applied to build Seokguram?

7. Why is the city of Gyeongju called a living museum?

③ 연등축제

고려시대 연등회에서 유래한 연등축제는 600년 역사를 자랑하는 한국의 전통축제이다. 매년 부처님오신날을 축하하기 위하여 음력 4월 8일을 전후하여 열린다. 연등은 지혜의 등불을 밝혀 이웃과 세상에 돕는 보살행을 하겠다는 마음을 상징한다. 한국의 연등축제는 매년 서울시청 앞 광장에 거대한 장엄등에 점등을 하면서 시작된다. 사전 행사로 호랑이, 용, 코끼리, 사천왕, 탑 등의 다양한 모양을 한 전통등의 전시회가 열린다.

특히 연등축제는 2012년 국가지정 무형문화재 제122호로 지정되어 불자들만의 축제가 아닌 전국민의 축제이자 전 세계인의 축제가 되었다. '불교문화마당'에서는 가족이 함께 와서 연등을 만들고, 불화도 그리고, 전통놀이를 체험할 수 있는 기회가 주어진다. 연등축제의 하이라이트를 장식하는 연등행렬이 펼쳐지는 밤에는 거대한 장엄등과 행렬 참가자의 손에 든 연등의 물결이 어두워진 서울 도심의 거리를 환히 밝힌다.

Unit 3 The Lotus Lantern Festival

Originating from the Goryeo Dynasty's Yeondeunghoe, the Lotus Lantern Festival is one of Korea's landmark traditional festivals which has a 600-year history. Every year, commemorating the birth of the Buddha, the festival starts around the 8th day of the 4th lunar month. Lotus lanterns symbolize the Buddhist vows to practice the bodhisattva path and help our neighbors and the world by lighting lanterns of wisdom. Korea's Lotus Lantern Festival starts with the lighting of the mega-sized "Grand Ornate Lantern" which is located in Seoul Plaza. As one of the pre-festival activities, Traditional Lantern Exhibitions are held showing beautifully adorned lanterns in the shapes of tigers, dragons, elephants, the four heavenly kings and pagodas.

In February 2012, the Korean government designated Yeondeunghoe as Important Intangible Cultural Heritage No. 122. This has made the Lotus Lantern Festival not only a nationwide festival for Koreans but also an international festival for all global citizens. The Buddhist Street Festival offers hands-on experiences for families such as making their own lotus lanterns, painting buddhas, and playing traditional games. On the night of the Lotus Lantern Parade, the highlight of the Lotus Lantern Festival, an ocean of grand ornate lanterns and colorful hand-held lanterns brighten up the streets of downtown Seoul.

Fill in the Blanks

1. The Lotus Lantern Festival is one of Korea's landmark _____ festivals which has a 600-year history. (전통)

2. Every year the festival starts around the 8th day of the 4th _____ month. (음력의)

3. Lotus lanterns symbolize the Buddhist _____ to practice the bodhisattva path. (서원)

4. Korea's Lotus Lantern Festival starts with the lighting of the _____ "Grand Ornate Lantern" which is located in Seoul Plaza. (거대한)

5. Traditional Lantern Exhibitions are held showing beautifully adorned lanterns in the shapes of tigers, _____, elephants, the four heavenly kings and _____. (용, 탑)

6. In February 2012, the Korean government designated Yeondeunghoe as Important _____ Cultural Heritage No. 122. (무형)

7. This has made the Lotus Lantern Festival not only a nationwide festival for Koreans but also an international festival for all _____ citizens. (세계의)

8. The Buddhist Street Festival offers _____ experiences for families. (직접적인)

9. On the night of the Lotus Lantern Parade, an ocean of grand ornate lanterns and colorful hand-held lanterns brighten up the streets of _____ Seoul. (도심)

Questions

1. Where does the Lotus Lantern Festival originate from?
2. What does the Lotus Lantern Festival commemorate?
3. What does a lotus lantern symbolize?
4. Which event marks the beginning of the Lotus Lantern Festival?
5. Can you find lanterns in the shapes of tigers or dragons at Traditional Lantern Exhibitions?
6. Yeondeunghoe is an Intangible Cultural Heritage of Korea?
7. Can you make your own lotus lanterns at the Buddhist Street Festival?

불교영어 초급2

1판 1쇄 펴냄 | 2012년 9월 1일
개정판 1쇄 펴냄 | 2015년 1월 30일
개정판 2쇄 펴냄 | 2019년 8월 20일

편찬 | 대한불교조계종 교육원 불학연구소
집필·번역 | 지엘통번역센터
총괄감수 | 진우기

발행인 | 정지현
편집인 | 박주혜
사장 | 최승천

펴낸곳 | (주)조계종출판사
출판등록 | 제2007-000078호(2007. 4. 27)
주소 | 서울시 종로구 삼봉로 81 두산위브파빌리온 232호
전화 | 02)720-6107~9
팩스 | 02)733-6708
구입문의 | 불교전문서점(www.jbbook.co.kr) 02)2031-2070~1

ISBN   978-89-93629-80-4 (세트)
         979-11-5580-033-1 04740

※ 본문 중 캐릭터와 사진 일부는 한국불교문화사업단에서 제공하였습니다.